T0328650

# Cambridge Elements ☰

**Elements in Business Strategy**
edited by
J.-C. Spender
*Kozminski University*

# BLOCKCHAINS

## *Strategic Implications for Contracting, Trust, and Organizational Design*

Wenqian Wang
*Purdue University*

Fabrice Lumineau
*The University of Hong Kong*

Oliver Schilke
*The University of Arizona*

Shaftesbury Road, Cambridge CB2 8EA, United Kingdom

One Liberty Plaza, 20th Floor, New York, NY 10006, USA

477 Williamstown Road, Port Melbourne, VIC 3207, Australia

314–321, 3rd Floor, Plot 3, Splendor Forum, Jasola District Centre,
New Delhi – 110025, India

103 Penang Road, #05–06/07, Visioncrest Commercial, Singapore 238467

Cambridge University Press is part of Cambridge University Press & Assessment,
a department of the University of Cambridge.

We share the University's mission to contribute to society through the pursuit of
education, learning and research at the highest international levels of excellence.

www.cambridge.org
Information on this title: www.cambridge.org/9781009060738

DOI: 10.1017/9781009057707

First published 2022

*A catalogue record for this publication is available from the British Library.*

ISBN 978-1-009-06073-8 Paperback
ISSN 2515-0693 (online)
ISSN 2515-0685 (print)

# Blockchains

## Strategic Implications for Contracting, Trust, and Organizational Design

Elements in Business Strategy

DOI: 10.1017/9781009057707
First published online: September 2022

Wenqian Wang
*Purdue University*

Fabrice Lumineau
*The University of Hong Kong*

Oliver Schilke
*The University of Arizona*

Author for correspondence: Wenqian Wang, wang4106@purdue.edu

**Abstract:** Blockchains have become increasingly important for organizing contemporary economic and social activities. This Element offers a deeper understanding of blockchains to both management scholars and practitioners, with an emphasis on blockchains' strategic implications for fundamental issues in organizing. It provides a critical examination of core themes, theoretical lenses, and methodologies used in blockchain research in business and management scholarship. Furthermore, it offers an in-depth discussion of why and how blockchains offer a new way of organizing, providing profound implications for three major issues of strategic organization: contracting, trust, and organizational design. It also discusses several limitations of the technology in its current stage of development. Finally, this Element points to the implication of blockchains on both scholarly research and business practice.

**Keywords:** blockchains, contracting, governance, organizational design, trust

ISBNs: 9781009060738 (PB), 9781009057707 (OC)
ISSNs: 2515-0693 (online), 2515-0685 (print)

# Contents

1 Introduction   1

2 Blockchain Fundamentals and Features   3

3 Extant Knowledge from Management Research   11

4 Blockchains as a New Way of Organizing   24

5 Critiques and Pitfalls   38

6 Conclusions and Implications   46

References   59

# 1 Introduction

For more than a decade, blockchains have been a buzzword permeating the business press, where they are often presented as a 'revolution'. Aside from this media attention, blockchains are now becoming a reality for an increasing number of organizations. Expanding beyond their roots in cryptocurrencies, blockchains have found their way into a broad range of industries, from retailing to insurance. Blockchains are starting to truly change the business world, and their impact on the global economy will likely only continue to grow over the coming decades. The number of blockchain-based projects has been rapidly increasing year by year. Deloitte's global blockchain surveys in 2019 and 2020 show that the percentage of companies that have already employed blockchains has increased nearly twofold, growing from 23 per cent in 2019 to 39 per cent in 2020 (Deloitte, 2020, p. 7). This percentage is even higher among large enterprises (46 per cent in the 'more than US$1 billion' revenue sector). Based on the technology's prospective usage across industries, a recent report by PwC shows that 'blockchain technology has the potential to boost global gross domestic product (GDP) by US$1.76 trillion over the next decade' (PwC, 2020, p. 4).

Blockchains have the potential to fundamentally disrupt the way in which business is conducted. They provide a new way of solving elemental business problems related to recording, tracking, verifying, and aggregating various types of information (Felin & Lakhani, 2018). Successful cases of blockchains abound in a variety of industries. The insurance industry benefits from blockchain-based fraud detection, record reconciliation, and risk prevention (CBInsights, 2019). In the energy sector, blockchains have been used to track and certify low-carbon energy and to enable direct transactions of energy between individuals, neighbourhoods, and even smart devices such as solar panels (Brink, 2021). Banks use blockchain technology to automate financial processes (e.g., transaction settlements and the issuance of credits and guarantees), create trustworthy auditable trails, and enhance the security of their systems (Garg et al., 2021). The auto industry has employed blockchains to trace parts across a vehicle's life cycle (Zavolokina et al., 2020). In the used car market, blockchains help track and immutably record information about vehicles, such as service history, mileage, and age (Gaszcz, 2019). Pharmaceutical companies employ blockchains to authenticate pharmaceutical products and prevent counterfeits from entering the supply chain (Mattke et al., 2019). Healthcare providers use blockchains to streamline information management systems and improve the interoperability of healthcare databases (Tanwar et al., 2020). For media companies, blockchains provide an attractive solution to help fight fabricated information and ensure the authenticity of news releases (Lacity & van Hoek, 2021b).

Consider *DL Freight* as one example of a blockchain that facilitates more efficient supply chains (for more details about the case, see Lacity & van Hoek, 2021a). DL Freight was initiated by Walmart Canada and DLT Labs, a company developing enterprise blockchain solutions. The major purpose of DL Freight is to drastically reduce the need for reconciling inconsistent information across the supply chain. Before implementing the blockchain, Walmart Canada had to incur significant costs to verify carriers' charges and to address disputes with them, and carriers complained about lengthy waiting times before receiving payments. The DL Freight blockchain aims to eliminate costly reconciliation processes by providing a single version of the truth in a reliable manner. Instead of validating and recording freight invoices and payments ex post, the DL Freight blockchain enables validation, recording, and sharing in real time. It uses smart contracts (i.e., preprogrammed codes that execute once certain conditions are met) to automatically produce invoices, issue reimbursements for late shipments, and process payments. Such automated actions are taken based on information collected by digital devices, such as GPS trackers on the truck, to determine the location of the freight. Consequently, the relevant data are transparent to authorized users, who share a common understanding of information for which agreements have been reached. Following the implementation of DL Freight, disputes regarding invoices reportedly decreased from 70 per cent to less than 2 per cent, and relationship satisfaction among supply chain participants significantly improved (Lacity & van Hoek, 2021a).

The above real-life examples of contemporary blockchain applications show that the technology can add value to a broad range of business activities. However, what are blockchains, and what makes them so different from other technologies? What changes will blockchains truly bring about, especially with regard to the strategic management of organizations? In this Element, we provide a critical assessment of the status quo as well as identify potential challenges and opportunities associated with blockchains. We especially highlight how blockchains can address a range of organizational issues related to both cooperation and coordination. Our core thesis is that blockchains can help firms overcome these enduring organizational challenges in a new way that cannot be fully replicated by traditional solutions. We show that blockchains may significantly change the way we think about traditional contracting and trust issues while offering novel opportunities in terms of organizational design.

In the next section, we start by outlining the history of blockchains and the fundamental features that make them stand out as a digital innovation that is poised to impact an increasingly broad range of organizations. After explaining what blockchains are, we turn our attention to decentralization as the most salient property that makes them stand out from other technologies, along with some resulting properties (i.e., immutability, data integrity, transparency, and tokenization), and to smart contracts as a key value-adding complementary feature. In Section 3, we provide an overview of the existing knowledge of blockchains in the management literature, outlining the central research themes of different management disciplines and the major theoretical lenses and methodologies employed. In Section 4, we focus on discussing the implications of blockchains for three important strategic issues, namely, contracting, trust, and organizational design. Blockchains are, of course, not without limitations. In Section 5, we direct our attention to some potential problems associated with blockchains and elaborate on important technical, ethical, regulatory, and environmental challenges. In Section 6, we conclude this study with a discussion of the implications of blockchains for both managers and academics.

## 2 Blockchain Fundamentals and Features

### 2.1 A Brief History

Although 2008, when the Bitcoin whitepaper was released, is often seen as the starting point of blockchain technology, the idea of a cryptographically secured chain of blocks for storing information can be traced back to Haber and Stornetta in 1991. In fact, the blockchains we see today are essentially an innovative integration of many technologies that date years, and even decades, earlier (Narayanan & Clark, 2017). In 2008, Satoshi Nakamoto (a pseudonym) introduced Bitcoin, a cryptocurrency that can be securely traded among users without a trusted party coordinating the exchange. In the years that followed, blockchains were primarily developed to support different types of cryptocurrencies, with limited other functionalities. These blockchains are often called the first generation. Going beyond monetary systems, a second generation of blockchains started to emerge, of which the Ethereum blockchain was the leader. Ethereum uses a different programming language, which supports smart contracts and more complex decentralized applications. This feature represents an important advancement because it allows people to code complex tasks into blockchain systems. Blockchains have thus been implemented in different industries with a variety of functionalities, as illustrated by the multiple examples presented earlier. To date, developers have devoted their attention to improving earlier versions of blockchain technology by solving existing drawbacks, such as poor scalability and interoperability. These newer developments are also referred to as the third generation of blockchains, among which the Cardano blockchain emerged as a leader. Next, we will explain the technology in greater detail.

## 2.2 Definitions

Given the relative novelty of blockchains, no consensual definition has emerged thus far. Influenced by the interest and focus on blockchains, practitioners and academics have suggested a variety of conceptualizations. We list some of the prominent attempts at defining blockchains in Table 1.

Based on the commonalities among extant conceptualizations, we propose the following integrative definition: blockchains are cryptography-based decentralized and distributed systems consisting of an ongoing list of digital records that are shared within a peer-to-peer network. This definition aims to capture the most general and fundamental features of blockchains while striving for conciseness.

A blockchain network contains different types of participants called nodes. A node can be any type of device, such as a computer, laptop, or server, with the

**Table 1** Different definitions of blockchains in the literature

| Literature | Definition of blockchains |
| --- | --- |
| Babich & Hilary (2020, p. 224) | 'A family of technologies used to develop and maintain distributed ledgers (i.e., databases that are massively replicated on all the "nodes" or machines in the system)' |
| Chod et al. (2020, p. 4379) | 'Blockchains are cryptographically secure, distributed ledgers that can enable decentralized verifiability of digital-goods transactions' |
| Cole et al. (2019, p. 470) | 'Blockchain is, essentially, a distributed database system that records transactional data or other information, secured by cryptography and governed by a consensus mechanism' |
| Du et al. (2019, p. 51) | 'A blockchain is a chain of data blocks each of which is created to record a transaction' |
| Pazaitis et al. (2017, p. 109) | 'A blockchain is a distributed ledger or database of transactions recorded in a distributed manner, by a network of computers' |
| Saberi et al. (2019, p. 2118) | 'Blockchain technology is a distributed database of records or shared public/private ledgers of all digital events that have been executed and shared among blockchain participating agents' |
| Treiblmaier (2018, p. 547) | 'The blockchain [is] a digital, decentralized and distributed ledger in which transactions are logged and added in chronological order with the goal of creating permanent and tamperproof records' |

required hardware (e.g., internet access) and software to be connected with other nodes. Blockchains operate in peer-to-peer networks, which refer to the architecture where every node has equal privilege and can exchange data and resources directly with each other. This design is different from the traditional client–server architecture, where information needs to pass through servers to be transmitted. Blockchains involve a number of previous advancements in cryptography, such as public–private key encryption, hash encryption, and digital signatures, integrating them in an innovative way to ensure information security (see Narayanan & Clark, 2017 for a discussion of the technical details of blockchains).

From a process perspective, a blockchain works as follows (see Figure 1). A participant in the network requests a new transaction, which is broadcast to other nodes in the network. Based on a certain consensus mechanism (i.e., the protocol based on which the nodes agree with each other), some nodes collectively verify whether the received transaction request is legitimate. Once verified, the transaction is added to the blockchain, usually in the form of a block with several pieces of records aggregated together. New blocks will be attached to the existing blocks by using hashes (i.e., one-way mathematical functions that map data of any size to data of a fixed size). Finally, the updated chain of information is broadcast to the network, indicating the complete execution of the transaction request.

Beyond the general features discussed in this section, note that individual blockchains can differ markedly from one another in terms of design, data structure, and consensus mechanisms, among other features (Werbach, 2018). The most frequently used way to categorize blockchains is the distinction

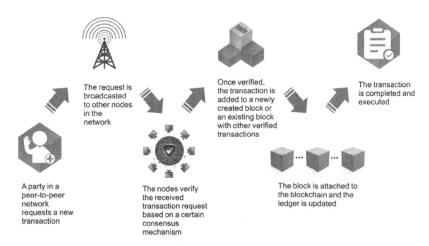

**Figure 1** The functioning of blockchains (Lumineau et al., 2021a)

between public and private blockchains, sometimes also referred to as permissionless and permissioned blockchains. In public/permissionless blockchains, any node with access to the Internet can participate in viewing and verifying information. Bitcoin and Ethereum are examples of such blockchains. In private/permissioned blockchains, only participants with permissions can participate in viewing and verifying transactions. Many enterprise blockchains aiming to be integrated and utilized for enterprise usages take this form, such as IBM's Hyperledger and R3's Corda. Some scholars further clarify the nuances of the differences by disentangling the right to read and submit transactions (public vs. private) from the right to validate transactions (permissionless vs. permissioned) (e.g., Beck et al., 2018). In fact, while different blockchains resemble each other to certain degrees, they also differ in many aspects of both design and performance (see the discussion of different consensus mechanisms in the next section). The term 'blockchain' has to date been used as an umbrella term to refer to a number of distributed ledger technologies by different parties (Narayanan & Clark, 2017). In this Element, our definition aims to distil the central features that generalize across most types of blockchains, whereas our discussion of blockchain features addresses the diversity in blockchain solutions.

Just as the Internet supports the direct exchange of information, a key objective of blockchains is to support the direct exchanges of value between independent parties, which traditionally happen through intermediaries (Lacity, 2020). For example, when people need to wirelessly transfer money to one another, banks are required to keep the record and make sure that the sender no longer possesses the value (i.e., cannot use the money) after sending it – also known as the double-spending problem. Blockchains can solve such problems without intermediaries, supporting their role in facilitating the direct exchange of value. To understand why they have this capability, we need to examine the critical functionalities enabled by blockchains. We start by considering decentralization, which is the most fundamental feature of blockchains.

## 2.3 Decentralization

By recombining a variety of technologies, including digital signatures and encryption methods, the most salient feature enabled by blockchains is arguably the decentralization of exchange networks (Hanisch et al., 2022). Blockchains enable a dispersion of rights to access information and make decisions (Vergne, 2020), which were traditionally held by trusted intermediaries (e.g., governments, banks, platform owners) through hierarchical lines.

Centralization has been the dominant approach to organization for manifold reasons, among which information consistency is particularly relevant.

Maintaining a consensual understanding of the status quo is important for any kind of collaborative relationship. For example, for financial systems, it is critical to keep information identical across different subsystems to avoid people arbitrarily withdrawing money from some accounts.

Generally, maintaining consensus tends to be easier for a centralized system than for a decentralized system. The central trusted party is tasked with verifying and distributing information, while others merely receive the information. In contrast, in decentralized systems where no such trusted party acts as a central coordinator, anyone can alter the information, and consensus is difficult to achieve and maintain.

Blockchains enable decentralization while maintaining information consistency through built-in consensus mechanisms. Put simply, consensus mechanisms define the voting rule among nodes and determine how the decisions to verify and add information to the blockchain are made in a way that all nodes agree on. Relevant consensus mechanisms range from proof-of-work (PoW), proof-of-stake (PoS), and practical Byzantine fault tolerant (PBFT) to lesser-known variants, such as proof-of-elapsed-time and proof-of-burn. There are also many hybrid consensus mechanisms, including proof-of-activity (hybrid of PoW and PoS) and proof-of-authority (hybrid of PoS and Byzantine fault tolerant) (Wang et al., 2019).

Consensus mechanisms are at the core of blockchains and reflect distinct blockchain designs. Each consensus mechanism has certain pros and cons and thus involves trade-offs across relevant performance dimensions of blockchains, including Byzantine fault tolerance, energy consumption, scalability, and the transaction rate. *Byzantine fault tolerance* refers to the maximum voting power of malicious nodes that the system can tolerate, which relates to the relative security of the system. Some consensus mechanisms, such as PoW and proof-of-elapsed-time, depend on a considerable number of computation tasks to allocate voting rights, which creates significant *energy consumption*. *Scalability* refers to the capacity of the system to accommodate a large number of participants. PBFT (and its variants), which is usually used in permissioned blockchains, often faces difficulties in attracting more participants to scale up. On the flip side, PBFT-based blockchains can maintain a high *transaction rate*, which represents the speed of reaching consensus and adding blocks. A comparison of different consensus mechanisms is presented in Table 2 (based on Bodkhe et al., 2020 and Wang et al., 2019).

A common theme that underlies all consensus mechanisms is their attempt to deliberately make it costly for any single party to unilaterally change the information on the system without drawing attention (Vergne, 2020). Hence, in blockchains, no single authority has full discretion in terms of verifying and updating records. Decentralization is thus a major merit of blockchains, as it can

**Table 2** A comparison of different consensus mechanisms

| | Proof-of-work | Proof-of-stake | Practical Byzantine fault tolerance | Proof-of-burn | Proof-of-elapsed-time | Proof-of-activity | Proof-of-authority |
|---|---|---|---|---|---|---|---|
| Basis of voting power | Based on the computational power to solve random puzzles | Based on the current monetary stake and random selection | Based on randomly selected orders | Based on the willingness to lose stake in the short term | Based on randomly assigned waiting times | Based on both computational power and the current monetary stake | Based on the nodes' reputation and random selection |
| Byzantine fault tolerance | 50 per cent | 50 per cent | ≤33 per cent | N/A | N/A | N/A | >50 per cent |
| Level of decentralization | High | High | Medium | High | Medium | High | Medium |
| Energy consumption | High | Low | Low | Low | High | High | Low |
| Scalability | High | High | Low | High | High | High | High |
| Transaction rate | Low | High | High | High | Medium | Low | High |

fundamentally alter the traditional paradigm of maintaining a consensual under-standing of the status quo according to which members of the system have to rely on a centralized party as the sole entity aggregating and holding informa-tion and making decisions.

## 2.4 Immutability, Data Integrity, Transparency, and Tokenization

The unique ability of blockchains to decentralize both access to information and decision-making rights lends blockchains a number of characteristics that make them attractive candidates for organizing a variety of important tasks. Centralized systems with a single point of failure are vulnerable to external malicious hacks, unexpected errors in the centralized authority's server, or even deliberate cheating by the central party. In contrast, blockchains are designed with the objective that no single party can change the recorded data without other parties noticing. The addition of new information to the blockchain requires a consensus among the nodes whose major task is verification, and the specific consensus mechanism is part of the protocol of the blockchain infrastructure. The system is thus resistant to the failure of individual nodes to the extent that even the system does not know exactly whether there is a failed component (Babich & Hilary, 2020). As long as the network has a majority of honest nodes that perform their tasks correctly and do not attempt to modify the transactional history, participants can have confidence that their transaction records are not corrupted.

In addition, blockchains allow identical information to be stored across different physical addresses (i.e., computers). This feature differs from most traditional digital systems, which concentrate information on a central server. Hacking then becomes more difficult because there is no centralized target to break into. Consequently, the information stored in blockchains is considered *immutable* and *censor resistant*, which further reinforces confidence in the *integrity of data* stored on blockchains.

The architecture of blockchains also greatly improves the *transparency* and *traceability* of the associated information. The information stored on blockchains is timestamped and linked chronologically. Depending on the protocol and purpose of the blockchain, participants have access to the information that they are supposed to see. Due to the immutability of blockchains, participants can easily trace the origin of digital assets or the source of information stored on blockchains, which makes blockchains particularly useful for supply chain man-agement (Saberi et al., 2019). Some examples include the Food Trust blockchain, which traces the logistical status of products across the actors of a food supply chain, and the Everledger blockchain, which traces and authenticates the origin of diamonds. The participants of these blockchains do not have to rely on cues and heuristics to judge potential value and risk along the supply chain but have a better understanding of the product due to the enhanced transparency and traceability supported by these blockchains (Montecchi et al., 2019).

The abovementioned properties of blockchains greatly enhance the value of *tokenization*, which refers to the process of converting assets, either physical or digital, into digital tokens on blockchains. Since digital artefacts (e.g., text, image, sound, numbers) can be easily copied and transmitted, it has been difficult to ensure that the original copy has been destroyed after being transferred to another party. Blockchains provide a decentralized solution that prevents the double-spending problem by ensuring that only one copy of the digital asset is valid. Such a design makes it possible to employ non-fungible tokens (NFTs) that are unique and cannot be replaced. For example, people may use an NFT to represent an artwork (Ennis, 2021). Since it is practically impossible to replicate the token, the NFT effectively provides authentication and certification of ownership of the artwork. Other examples of tokenization through blockchains include the trade of music ownership (Forde, 2021), the verification of data regarding carbon emission quotas (Kim & Huh, 2020), and the certification of land registry (Oprunenco & Akmeemana, 2018). The use of NFTs will change the way people portray their identities online (Segal, 2021).

## 2.5 Smart Contracts and Automation

Most blockchains rely on smart contracts to automatically execute transactions involving digital assets (Buterin, 2014). Smart contracts are lines of computer code that automatically execute whenever certain predefined conditions are met. Thus, smart contracts can greatly facilitate the automation of transactions. For example, a smart contract can be programmed to automate payments. To illustrate, as soon as a set of radio-frequency identification (RFID) chips reaches a dock, the smart contract automatically generates a receiving report and authorizes the payment (Yuthas et al., 2021).

The idea of smart contracts originated well before the invention of blockchains (Szabo, 1997). However, for the longest time, it failed to garner much popularity since it has always been possible to alter agreements unilaterally, leaving low-power parties vulnerable to changes. In contrast, blockchains have made it possible to make agreements immutable, a property that strongly complements smart contracts and ensures that the programs are intact and that the transaction conditions have not been tampered with (Narayanan & Clark, 2017).

Blockchains do not necessarily have smart contracts embedded. For example, the Bitcoin blockchain does not feature smart contracts. However, the use of smart contracts can greatly broaden the scope of blockchain applications in various areas. The programming language used by Ethereum allows an 'if . . . then . . . ' logic to be programmed into the code so that agreements can be executed automatically as a function of the status of certain conditions. This logic enables Ethereum to move beyond being a mere cryptocurrency to involve various types of decentralized applications, such as fundraising and identity management (Palmer, 2016). In turn, this capability is the major reason why the Ethereum blockchain differs from Bitcoin and is often referred to as belonging to the second generation of blockchains (e.g., Chen et al., 2020). In sum, although not every blockchain has smart contracts written into it, smart contracts are often seen as a salient functionality of blockchains that expands the spectrum of applications of blockchain technology through automation.

In this section, we have explained the meaning of blockchains and how they work. We also pointed to the most common and fundamental features that make the technology unique. Based on these features, we suggest that blockchains should be viewed as an institutional technology that far surpasses technical innovations. By truly leveraging digital technology's computational and data-based capabilities, blockchains have potentially vast social implications that may change how people interact with each other and how people conduct business. In the sections that follow, we will first review extant management research on blockchains. We will then turn to elaborating blockchains' impacts on key organizational processes, including contracting, trust, and organizational design.

## 3 Extant Knowledge from Management Research

Although blockchains are still a relatively new phenomenon in the early stage of development, scholarly enthusiasm has been substantial. While a large fraction of the academic research on blockchains has been conducted in the field of computer science, management scholars have started to show increasing interest in understanding blockchains' implications for organizations. To gain a detailed understanding of the state of the art of blockchain research in management, we conducted a systematic literature review. Specifically, on 5 May 2022, we searched the Web of Science Core Collection database for articles that contain the term 'blockchain' in their title. The search yielded a total of 11,951 hits, demonstrating significant scholarly interest ranging from the social sciences (sociology, anthropology, political science, etc.) to mathematics and engineering. A total of 710 of these articles came from the

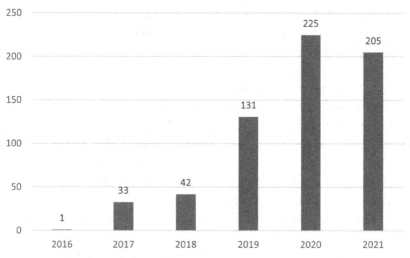

**Figure 2** Number of blockchain-related research articles covered by the business and management category of the Web of Science Core Collection database (no search results prior to 2016)

field of business and management. Figure 2 illustrates the growing research interest in blockchains within this field over time. In the following sections, we present an overview of the core themes in different management disciplines as well as associated theories, methodologies, and empirical evidence.

### 3.1 Core Themes in Blockchain Research across Management Disciplines

*Finance* is the area in business research that has paid the most attention to blockchains. This fact may not come as a surprise since blockchains were initially invented to power cryptocurrencies in financial technology (FinTech). Thus, scholars have aspired to understand various aspects of cryptocurrencies (e.g., Halaburda et al., 2020; Liu & Tsyvinski, 2021). One of the earliest studies on this topic is Wang and Vergne (2017), who find that the innovation potential reflected in technological upgrades is the major factor explaining a cryptocurrency's weekly returns. They also find that in the case of cryptocurrency, unlike traditional currencies, an increase in the supply is positively related to the weekly return. Such a finding leads the authors to conclude that cryptocurrencies behave quite differently from traditional currencies. Another exemplary study is Cennamo and colleagues (2020), who study the factors driving the success and volatility of cryptocurrencies. They find that due to significant network externalities, cryptocurrencies that are created on well-known third-party blockchains (compared to those on more specialized blockchains) attract higher value and are at the same time more volatile. There are also several studies devoted to describing and understanding the dynamics of the rise and fall of the prices and values of cryptocurrencies (e.g., Bouri et al., 2019; Fry & Cheah, 2016; Makarov & Schoar, 2020).

Of particular relevance to management scholarship, cryptocurrencies enable a new way of financing organizations, called the initial coin offering (ICO). An ICO differs from a traditional initial public offering (IPO) in that it directly connects entrepreneurs and investors through blockchain tokens (Adhami et al., 2018). ICO-based fundraising is thus thought to democratize access to capital, which has traditionally been limited to venture capitalists and angel investors (Chen, 2018). An ICO can be viewed as a mode of crowdfunding – broadly understood as raising small amounts of funds for new ventures from a large number of investors. However, ICOs differ from more centralized ways of crowdfunding through platforms, such as Kickstarter and Indiegogo, which rely on mediators to present the project details on a website and match donations with projects (Iftody, 2019). However, due to information asymmetries, it is often difficult to discern legitimate coins from cryptocurrency scams. For instance, Fisch and Momtaz (2020) show that institutional investors' superior screening and training abilities can help overcome the information asymmetry issue and increase the performance of ICO-financed ventures.

Blockchains may also have implications for financing strategies beyond cryptocurrencies. For example, due to the lack of trustworthy records of their credit and assets, small and medium-sized enterprises often need third-party guarantors to endorse their financing applications. This model creates additional risk for the guarantor and in turn poses additional costs to the borrowers. Blockchains may enable improvements by allowing borrowers to credibly mortgage their current assets without a third-party guarantor. In this way, small and medium-sized enterprises can essentially self-guarantee their financing applications. Yu and colleagues (2021) show that the blockchain-based financing model effectively reduces guarantee risk compared to the traditional model.

*Operations and supply chain management* (OSCM) is another area in which blockchains have attracted much scholarly attention, given that a large number of blockchains aim at coordinating different supply chain stages (Cole et al., 2019). Being primarily concerned with planning, organizing, and supervising in the contexts of the production, manufacturing, or provision of services, OSCM scholars have endeavoured to understand the value of blockchain adoption in improving supply chain performance. For instance, a direct advantage of the use of blockchains is an improved ability to track the provenance of goods transferred across the supply chain (Montecchi et al., 2019). In particular, Babich and Hilary (2020) find that there are several key benefits of deploying blockchains in operations management, including improved visibility throughout the entire supply chain, aggregation of information, verification, and authentication of information, automation in executing transactions, and resilience and fault tolerance.

A related stream of OSCM research examines the relationship between blockchains and the efficiency and sustainability of supply chain management (e.g., Bai & Sarkis, 2020; Saberi et al., 2019; Sulkowski, 2018; Tsolakis et al., 2021). For example, Saberi and colleagues (2019) argue that the adoption of blockchains facilitates the verification of the provenance of products across the whole supply chain, which ensures that processes, products, and activities comply with economic, social, and environmental objectives. For example, to limit the overgrazing of goats and improve the sustainability of cashmere production, the United Nations and Mongolia developed a blockchain-based app to track and identify cashmere from herders following sustainable practices (Huang, 2019).

Another topic of interest to OSCM researchers relates to the barriers and challenges of successful blockchain adoption in supply chain management (e.g., Saberi et al., 2019; van Hoek, 2019). For example, based on expert interviews and Delphi surveys, Kurpjuweit and colleagues (2021) identify important barriers when organizations try to integrate blockchain technologies with additive manufacturing (more commonly known as 3D printing) to ensure the authentication of digital information, such as digital design files and printing parameters. Such barriers include a lack of standards for protocols and interfaces of blockchains, difficulty in integrating blockchains with existing IT systems (e.g., ERP systems), compatibility between different blockchain systems, and privacy concerns.

Additionally, blockchains have attracted considerable research interest from scholars in *entrepreneurship and innovation*, given that blockchain innovations are often propagated by new ventures. For example, Chalmers and colleagues (2021) show that blockchains can be an important enabler of entrepreneurial ideas. These authors illustrate how blockchains bring new value propositions to the music industry, including disintermediating and using smart contracts to automate artists' royalty collections. Moreover, as mentioned above, ICOs provide a new way of attracting funding for start-ups. A survey shows that ICO projects had raised over $50 billion in funds worldwide as of November 2019 (Statista, 2021).

As an alternative way of fundraising, ICOs offer unique advantages that traditional approaches lack. For instance, compared to lengthy IPOs, ICOs can save considerable time. Compared to other approaches such as venture capital, ICOs broaden the pool of potential investors to virtually anyone around the world who has internet access. The case of modum.io, a Swiss start-up providing blockchain-based solutions to the problems of supply chain quality control in the pharmaceutical industry, vividly illustrates these benefits of ICOs (Huang et al., 2020). Despite tedious networking efforts and months of negotiations, raising enough money to fund their prize-winning initiative turned out to be extremely challenging. The management team of modum.io finally conducted an ICO to attract investments, which turned out to be highly successful. The ICO raised a total of US$13.5 million in only 22 days, involving 4,150 investors from different parts of the world.

Despite the fact that blockchains seem to be particularly suitable for facilitating transactions in the *international business* (IB) context, scholarly enquiries in this area are not yet pervasive (see also Chang et al., 2020b), with the exception of a recent special issue (Torres de Oliveira et al., 2020). In this issue, Hooper and Holtbrügge (2020) show that blockchains can effectively protect property rights and reduce transaction costs in IB, as well as increase customer welfare by enhancing transparency.

Another potentially promising direction in IB scholarship is studying the born global companies that practice IB from or near their founding. Blockchain-based start-ups are inherently born global since blockchain technology is open sourced and decentralized and virtually by their design can easily be distributed globally. As Zalan (2018) suggests, blockchains provide an opportunity to connect the literature on born global and the literature on the economics of information goods and platform economics to revisit important theories and concepts in IB, such as distance. Other scholars, focusing on IBs, examine the value of adopting blockchains in addressing some of these companies' critical problems, such as cross-border payments, the long lead time between shipping and delivery, and complex customs procedures (Liu & Li, 2020; Yoon et al., 2020). At the same time, in international transactions, blockchains may induce negative externalities, such as energy consumption to facilitate transactions, and given their transnational nature, give rise to complex regulatory issues (Hooper & Holtbrügge, 2020).

In addition to examining the advantages or barriers to the adoption of blockchain technologies in different managerial functional areas, both organization theory and management information system scholars have analysed the governance *of* blockchain-based organizations (e.g., Beck et al., 2018; Chen et al., 2021; Davidson et al., 2018; Schmeiss et al., 2019; Trabucchi et al., 2020; Ziolkowski et al., 2020). For example, Beck and colleagues (2018) suggest that the governance of blockchains should be examined along three dimensions: decision rights, accountability, and incentives. Decision rights can vary from centralized to decentralized, representing whether the power to make decisions

is concentrated in one single party or dispersed across many parties; accountability concerns the consequences of actions taken, which may vary from being
institution-enacted (based on the law or social relationships) to technology-
enacted (based on the technology); and incentives refer to the extent to which
the interests of participants are aligned with the general goal of the blockchain.
Another study by Goldsby and Hanisch (2022) recognizes challenges in both
controlling and coordinating participants' joint actions and identifies four
generic modes of governance of blockchains to address such challenges –
chief, clan, custodian, and consortium.

Along this line of enquiry, we contend that a fruitful research direction is to
investigate the performance implications of different governance decisions of
blockchain-based organizations. Current empirical evidence revolves around
decentralization as the core design choice of blockchains. Research has
produced mixed findings regarding the impact of the level of decentralization
on the performance of blockchains. In their nuanced analysis, Hsieh and
colleagues (2017) find differential effects of decentralization across layers
of blockchains. Decentralization of the voting power of the blockchain has a
positive effect on the returns of cryptocurrencies, indicating a general interest
from investors concerning the most important feature of blockchain technology. Additionally, having a centralized company steer the directions of the
blockchain is indeed beneficial for the performance of the cryptocurrency. For
example, while the Ripple blockchain is decentralized across nodes, it is
managed by the Ripple company, which actively hires developers and decides
the direction of code development. Chen and colleagues (2021) demonstrate
an inverted U-shaped impact, showing that excessive levels of decentralization can jeopardize market capitalization, developer attention, and the development activity of blockchain-based platforms. Table 3 summarizes the
central themes in blockchain research across management disciplines.

## 3.2 Theoretical Lenses for Examining Blockchains

To date, management research on blockchains has paid more attention to explaining the empirical phenomenon than to elaborating its theoretical bases and implications. In this section, we start to address this challenge and discuss the linkages of
blockchains with some of the most central theories in management, including
transaction cost economics, agency theory, and the resource-based view.

### 3.2.1 Transaction Cost Economics

*Transaction cost economics* is concerned mainly with minimizing the cost of
exchange (Williamson, 1985). Blockchains have the potential to reduce various

**Table 3** A summary of core themes in blockchain research across management disciplines

| Scholarly fields | Major research themes | Illustrative studies |
|---|---|---|
| Finance | • Dynamics of cryptocurrencies<br>• ICOs as a new way to finance organizations | E.g., Cong & He, 2019; Halaburda et al., 2020; Liu & Tsyvinski, 2021 |
| Operations and supply chain management | • Blockchains as new solutions to supply chain management problems (e.g., traceability and product authentication)<br>• Blockchains and the sustainability of supply chain management<br>• Barriers to blockchain adoption in supply chains | E.g., Cole et al., 2019; Kurpjuweit et al., 2021; Saberi et al., 2019 |
| Entrepreneurship and innovation | • Blockchain-related innovative ideas and new ventures<br>• ICOs as a new way to finance new ventures | E.g., Allen et al., 2020; Chalmers et al., 2021; Huang et al., 2020 |
| International business | • Blockchains as new solutions to reducing high transactions costs due to distance<br>• Blockchain-based born global organizations | E.g., Torres de Oliveira et al., 2020; Yoon et al., 2020; Zalan, 2018 |
| Organizational theory | • Blockchains as new ways of organizing<br>• The governance of blockchain-based organizations | E.g., Hsieh et al., 2017; Lumineau et al., 2021a; Murray et al., 2021a |
| Management information systems | • The governance of blockchain-based organizations | E.g., Beck et al., 2018; van Pelt et al., 2021; Ziolkowski et al., 2020 |

types of transaction costs (e.g., Ahluwalia et al., 2020; Pereira et al., 2019; Schmidt & Wagner, 2019). An early study by Catalini and Gans (2016) argues that two key types of transaction costs are directly impacted by blockchains: the cost of verification and the cost of networking. On the one hand, blockchains can enable participants to more efficiently verify and audit transaction attributes (e.g., the authenticity of the product or the state of ownership). Traditionally, this function has been performed by intermediaries (e.g., the government verifies the identity of a citizen, and banks verify the ownership of money), which creates additional costs for the transacting parties (e.g., charging a fee and accessing private data). Blockchains remove the need for intermediaries and replace them with a decentralized method of verification, thus reducing the cost of verification. On the other hand, to achieve the benefits of networking (i.e., to bootstrap the size of an economic network), the traditional approach has again relied on a centralized entity, which unavoidably introduces concentrated market power. Blockchains can realize networking without introducing the concentrated market power of a certain entity, thus reducing the cost of networking.

Lumineau and colleagues (2021a) extend this line of enquiry by examining how blockchains impact costs across different stages of a transaction. Transaction costs can be categorized as *ex ante* transaction costs, including the cost of searching for a partner and designing the agreement, and *ex post* transaction costs, including the cost of monitoring partners' behaviours and enforcing agreements. Blockchains are likely to reduce transaction costs in the searching, monitoring, and enforcing stages. However, they tend to generate higher design costs because using blockchains requires codifying transaction requirements into computer code, which is usually costlier than using natural language to represent agreements. We will return to these issues in Section 6.1.

### 3.2.2 Agency Theory

*Agency theory* is interested in the issues that occur when one person or entity (an 'agent') is able to make decisions and/or take actions on behalf of another person or entity (a 'principal') (Jensen & Meckling, 1976). In this principal–agent relationship, the principal needs to delegate decision-making power to the agent, who has better local information and a superior capability to address certain problems. However, given information asymmetries and misaligned interests, the principal also needs to incentivize, monitor, and control the agent's behaviour. Research suggests that by providing a transparent information recording system, blockchains can enable information flows accessible to both the principal and the agent (Treiblmaier, 2018). Proprietary information that was traditionally exclusive to the agents is now also accessible to the principals (e.g., status of the products in a supply chain). Therefore, blockchains can reduce the level of information asymmetry, which in turn may lower the necessity for the principal to exert excessive controlling efforts, lessening the threat of agency problems (Murray et al., 2021a).

### 3.2.3 Resource-based View

The resource-based view (RBV) defines organizations as heterogeneous bundles of resources, including assets and capabilities. The core thesis of the RBV is that organizations that possess valuable and rare resources can obtain a competitive advantage and that if the resources are further inimitable and nonsubstitutive (VRIN), these organizations may enjoy a sustained competitive advantage over competitors (Barney, 1991). Examining blockchains from the perspective of the RBV, Treiblmaier (2018) argues that the capability to use smart contracts to automate certain processes can represent such a resource. By introducing a new set of capabilities and obsoleting some traditional ones, 'blockchain technology thus bears the potential to fundamentally alter the importance of (critical) resources for sustained advantage across industries' (Treiblmaier, 2018, p. 552). Sundarakani and colleagues (2021) contend that integrating big data analytics and blockchains can help firms build VRIN resources that help them compete in Industry 4.0.

Following a similar logic, Nandi and colleagues (2020) find that by integrating blockchains into their supply chains, firms can leverage several capabilities to enhance their performance. Specifically, these authors indicate that blockchains are more likely to enhance a firm's operational-level capabilities (e.g., information sharing and coordination capabilities) than its strategic-level capabilities (e.g., integration and collaboration capabilities). In contrast, Yuthas and colleagues (2021) contend that blockchains can be equally useful in contributing to firms' strategic capabilities and enhancing their competitive advantage. Viewing blockchains as a specific type of strategic alliance, these authors argue that blockchain participants can improve their existing capabilities, share complementary capabilities, and build new capabilities that are blockchain-specific (e.g., smart contract expertise and blockchain implementation). These capabilities may in turn help consolidate participants' competitive advantage. In sum, blockchains may shift the sources of competitive advantage such that organizations that make effective use of blockchain technology may enjoy superior performance. The detailed mechanisms and conditions under which this competitive advantage occurs should provide numerous opportunities for future RBV research on blockchains.

### 3.2.4 Other Theoretical Perspectives

While we also identified other theoretical perspectives employed to study blockchains, the number of such perspectives is relatively sparse. Nonetheless, some of them are worth mentioning. For example, Nandi and colleagues (2021) examine blockchains by using the *resource dependency theory*. Building on the premise that firm performance depends on the external environment from which it acquires resources, they find that firms with superior blockchain expertise may reduce their resource dependence (i.e., gain more control over resources and lessen their dependence on other firms). In turn, these firms are in a better position to build resilience-related capabilities to respond to supply chain disturbances, resulting in better firm performance.

Furthermore, Chen and colleagues (2021) leverage the *mechanism design theory* to examine the optimal level of decentralization of blockchain-based digital platforms. Building on the thesis that 'an effective governance structure should leverage individual incentives and local information to achieve desirable outcomes' (p. 2), they argue (and empirically show) that a moderately high level of decentralization is optimal to achieve incentive compatibility and desirable governance outcomes.

*Game theory* may also be applied to the analysis of blockchains. Developing a prisoner's dilemma-like game-theoretical model, Mohan (2019) shows that blockchains can potentially address academic misconduct by realizing decentralized cooperation through incentivizing the monitoring of academic output and trust building.

Finally, Park and colleagues (2020) look at blockchain-based start-ups through the lens of *industrial economics* and zoom in on first-mover advantage acting as a profit driver. Somewhat counterintuitively, they suggest that a first-mover advantage may not exist in regard to attracting funding from venture capitalists and that moving early may also bring competitive disadvantages to blockchain start-ups. This reasoning is plausible because the blockchain industry is characterized by open innovation; therefore, active knowledge transfer and spillover are common. Firms disclose the technology through whitepapers and open-source software codes, which introduces the possibility of imitation by competitors. Considering these conditions, this reasoning suggests an inverted U-shaped relationship between entry timing and the performance of blockchain start-ups.

In sum, there is significant potential for management research on blockchains to go beyond describing specific cases to identify stylized facts and progressively develop generalizable theory. Extant analyses of blockchains have remained largely focused on a limited number of disciplinary and theoretical approaches (see Table 4 for a summary). While finance and OSCM research has made notable contributions to the current knowledge of blockchains, scholars in organizational behaviour, accounting, marketing (see Gleim & Stevens, 2021 for a preliminary discussion of blockchains' implications for marketing research), and strategy have paid relatively scant attention to blockchains and their implications. Similarly, our systematic review of the literature did not

**Table 4** A summary of selected theoretical lenses for examining blockchains

| Theory | Relation to blockchain research | Illustrative studies |
|---|---|---|
| Transaction cost economics | Blockchains have implications for reducing certain types of transaction costs at different stages of the transaction | E.g., Catalini & Gans, 2016; Lumineau et al., 2021a |
| Agency theory | Blockchains have implications for reducing certain types of agency costs within organizations | E.g., Murray et al., 2021a |
| Resource-based view | Blockchain-related resources and capabilities can generate competitive advantages for organizations | E.g., Nandi et al., 2020; Yuthas et al., 2021 |
| Resource dependency theory | Superior blockchain-related resources generate resource dependence strength for organizations | E.g., Nandi et al., 2021 |
| Mechanism design theory | The optimal level of decentralization of blockchain-based digital platforms is an important and highly contingent variable | E.g., Chen et al., 2021 |
| Game theory | Blockchains can change the payoff structures and behaviours of economic players | E.g., Mohan, 2019 |
| Industrial economics | The timing of blockchain adoption is a relevant strategic decision that has to balance the trade-offs between first-mover advantages and disadvantages | E.g., Park et al., 2020 |

identify any articles leveraging some central theories in management and organization, such as the behavioural theory of the firm, institutional theory, knowledge-based view theory, real options theory, or stakeholder theory. For instance, stakeholder theory could provide a relevant theoretical framework to analyse the conflicting demands resulting from the diversity of stakeholders involved in blockchains (ranging from IT developers, consumers, regulators, and local governments) and the ensuing tensions among these multiple constituencies. These blind spots open up fruitful avenues for future research. Connecting blockchains with classical theories is likely to significantly improve our understanding of the disruptive nature of the technology. Of course, new theoretical frameworks should also be considered to illuminate the unique features of blockchains.

## 3.3 Methodologies and Empirical Evidence

Scholars who are developing an interest in blockchains might be wondering how to conduct empirical research on a phenomenon that is only emerging. To provide some guidance, this section presents some of the major methodologies used in blockchain research to date, along with the relevant empirical evidence. We discuss the current use of formal modelling techniques, qualitative studies, and quantitative methods in blockchain research.

Several scholars have proposed formal analytical models to analyse blockchains (e.g., Cai et al., 2021; Chod et al., 2020; Cong & He, 2019; Mohan, 2019; Yoon et al., 2020). This methodological approach is most commonly employed by finance and operations management scholars to analyse the benefits of blockchains for managing economic activities and to identify the optimal design of blockchains. For example, Chod and colleagues (2020) demonstrate that by making supply chains more transparent, blockchains can help signal a firm's fundamental capabilities (such as operational capabilities). They further show that signalling through blockchains is more efficient than other signalling approaches (e.g., signalling through loan requests) and that such efficiency gains are a function of a firm's operational characteristics (e.g., operating cost, market size, and inventory salvage value). Another example comes from the study by Cong and He (2019), who show that decentralized consensus mechanisms alter the information environment by reducing information asymmetries between transacting parties. This effect, in turn, has many-faceted implications for the equilibria of economic activities, including lowering entry barriers, facilitating greater competition, and enhancing consumer surplus and social welfare.

In terms of empirical approaches, qualitative case studies are the most popular research method adopted by scholars, which is not surprising given the newness of the phenomenon and the current development stage of blockchain technology, as qualitative research typically involves gathering in-depth insights into a problem or generating new ideas for research. The overall existing empirical evidence is largely explorative in nature. This trend may also be explained by the absence of any databases for the purpose of conducting large-scale structured quantitative investigations.

Many qualitative studies approach the phenomenon through detailed investigations into a successfully deployed blockchain project (e.g., Du et al., 2019; Sternberg et al., 2021). As an illustration, Pazaitis and colleagues (2017) study the value of blockchain technology in supporting social sharing and peer production through a blockchain-based decentralized network community, which enables users to evaluate the contribution of each other and collectively verify the produced value and the distribution of rewards. They demonstrate that blockchains can provide a decentralized record of value, which helps to determine the value of the contributions to peer production.

There are also some qualitative investigations that involve multiple cases. For example, comparing two blockchain-based peer-to-peer electricity trading projects, Hojckova and colleagues (2020) find that the wide diffusion of decentralized blockchains is all but a given and depends on incumbents who own and manage the physical grid infrastructure. Other studies employ qualitative comparative analysis (QCA) to examine cross-case patterns. For example, Clohessy and Acton (2019) use QCA to study the organizational factors impacting blockchain adoption. They find that blockchain awareness, top management support, organization size, and organizational readiness are among the most important determinants.

While large-scale quantitative studies are not yet abundant, there are some exceptions that build on archival data and provide some preliminary evidence concerning firm-level performance implications of blockchain adoption. For example, using panel data of publicly listed firms in China, Hasan and colleagues (2020) demonstrate a positive change in firms' operational efficiency in the years after blockchain deployment compared to the year before blockchain deployment. Using data from several cryptocurrency networks, Alabi (2017) estimated several growth models to determine whether blockchain-based networks follow Metcalfe's law, which states that the value of a network is proportional to the square of its nodes. The results demonstrate that the value of blockchain networks is indeed related to the number of active users, in support of a strong network effect.

Scholars also use stock market data and event-study approaches to estimate the impact of blockchain-related events on firms' stock market performance (e.g., Akyildirim et al., 2020; Jain & Jain, 2019; Sharma et al., 2020). In an exemplary study, Cheng and colleagues (2019) show that describing blockchain-related activities (e.g., a plan of adopting blockchains in firm operations or a description of a blockchain product) in a firm's 8-K disclosure is related to positive stock market returns from investors. The study further shows that the magnitude of such positive returns is correlated with the Bitcoin price at the time of the event window, suggesting an overreaction of investors to blockchain technology.

Surveys are also a useful approach to acquire data for studying blockchains (e.g., Liang et al., 2021), especially when studying subjective phenomena, such as perceptions, intentions, and satisfaction. One example is the study by Kamble and colleagues (2019), who collected data through 181 questionnaires. They find that perceived usefulness (rather than perceived ease of use) is the key factor impacting the adoption of blockchain technology. Similarly, Yang (2019) leveraged a survey to study a maritime shipping supply chain and showed that improved customs clearance, digitizing and easing paperwork, standardization, and platform development are among the major factors positively impacting managers' intent to adopt blockchains.

In conclusion, we find that blockchains are attracting increasing interest among management scholars using a variety of methodologies (see Table 5 for a summary). Empirical studies are still mainly in the exploratory stage, relying on inductive studies derived from qualitative case study data. Performance outcomes remain difficult to observe, partly because a large number of blockchain-based solutions are still in the proof-of-concept stage. Apart from a few exceptions, quantitative studies have remained relatively rare thus far. Our review did not find blockchain studies that conducted experiments, indicating that scholars have yet to leverage the full suite of methodological options to address new questions and to provide unique insights in the field of blockchain research.

## 4 Blockchains as a New Way of Organizing

Our literature review above shows that despite their recent emergence, blockchains have already attracted much attention among management scholars, who seem to agree that blockchains have important implications for organizations. Building on and extending what has been discussed in the extant literature, we argue that the most noticeable innovation that blockchains offer is a new way of organizing collaborations both between and within organizations. We provide

**Table 5** A summary of methodologies for examining blockchains

| Method | Dominant research approaches | Illustrative studies |
|---|---|---|
| Formal modelling | • Modelling the impact of blockchains on economic equilibria | E.g., Cai et al., 2021; Chod et al., 2020; Cong & He, 2019 |
| Qualitative studies | • Detailed investigations into one blockchain case<br>• Cross-case comparison among multiple blockchains | E.g., Clohessy & Acton, 2019; Du et al., 2019; Pazaitis et al., 2017 |
| Quantitative studies | • Collecting archival data (e.g., cryptocurrency prices and stock market data)<br>• Conducting surveys to collect first-hand information | E.g., Cheng et al., 2019; Hasan et al., 2020; Kamble et al., 2019 |

a brief background on collaborations in organizational settings before elaborating how blockchains may impact their mechanics.

Collaboration can be defined as an activity in which a group of autonomous entities engage in an interactive process to complete a task or achieve a goal (Wood & Gray, 1991). Across levels of analysis, forms of collaboration can range from individuals working together on a production task to firms cooperating in a strategic alliance to develop a new vaccine to nations engaging in trade or defence agreements. Building on the premise that a group of people working together can oftentimes create more value than the sum of them working individually, collaboration is the foundation of wealth creation. This rationale is deeply rooted in Adam Smith's (1776) seminal explanation of the wealth of nations, emphasizing the necessity of the specialization and division of labour.

Collaborations are undoubtedly critical for the routine functioning of organizations. Individual departments and work groups need to work closely with each other to pursue the common goals of the organization. Frontline employees perform tasks together with co-workers. Managers collaborate with employees to monitor and steer their efforts. Organizations also frequently collaborate with one another to create value, forming partnerships to co-perform certain activities, such as research and development (R&D) (Sampson, 2007; Schilke & Goerzen, 2010) or production and distribution (Roels & Tang, 2017), or to learn from one another (Khanna et al., 1998).

However, collaboration usually does not come easily and often fails. Limitations in human nature create significant obstacles impeding a systematic and full realization of the benefits of collaboration. In particular, collaboration raises both cooperation and coordination issues (Gulati et al., 2012). On the one hand, humans are likely to behave opportunistically, meaning that they may pursue self-interest with guile (Williamson, 1985). Due to misaligned interests, collaborating partners may deliberately lie, cheat, shirk, or twist information to misguide their counterparts for the purpose of benefitting themselves. Opportunism can lead to cooperation failures, which not only damage the returns of already made inputs but also disincentivize future investments and efforts from collaborating parties.

On the other hand, humans have limited cognitive abilities. Consequently, they tend to behave rationally but with a limited capacity, which is also referred to as bounded rationality. According to Herbert Simon (1957), three factors contribute to bounded rationality: the limited information processing capacity of human brains, the limited time for decision-making, and the limited information available. As such, even the most honest collaborators face the risk of coordination failures. They may experience difficulty communicating their task divisions, mutual expectations, information at hand, or work progress.

Therefore, to ensure successful collaboration, actors need to carefully organize and govern their relationships. Contracts and relational norms are the most commonly employed governance mechanisms to both safeguard the relationship from opportunism and to facilitate coordination (Malhotra & Lumineau, 2011; Poppo & Zenger, 2002). Management and organization scholars have conducted a broad array of studies to understand how the design and management of contractual and relational mechanisms impact the effectiveness and efficiency of collaborations (e.g., Li et al., 2010; Ryall & Sampson, 2009; Schilke & Lumineau, 2018). In their comprehensive meta-analysis, Cao and Lumineau (2015) listed no fewer than 149 empirical articles related to this central issue.

In addition to the specific contractual and relational governance mechanisms, organizational design can also substantially impact collaborative outcomes. Well-designed organizational structures can support the distribution of tasks and responsibilities, assign accountability, and enable rapid responses to opportunities and threats. In contrast, if organizational design is not aligned with the goals of the organization, negative consequences are likely to occur, such as the inability to meet these goals and to address pressure for change, which can ultimately jeopardize the organization's survival (Puranam, 2018). Most formal organizations are centrally managed. While this mode of organization presents advantages, problems also prevail, such as failures to mobilize resources, coordinate efforts, share information, and incentivize employees.

In this Element, we argue that a core merit of blockchains is that they allow for new ways to organize collaborations by altering key aspects of organizational contracts, trust, and design. Specifically, we propose that block-chains offer a fundamentally new approach to collaboration that enforces agreements automatically through codes and algorithms, representing a method that is substantially different from the traditional contractual approach. Blockchains also change several important aspects of organizational trust, including its nature, mode of production, and targets. Finally, blockchains affect organizational design by enabling new modes of organizing that might go as far as obliterating the need for managers altogether, such as in the extreme case of decentralized autonomous organizations (DAOs).

## 4.1 Blockchains and Contracting

In what follows, we address the interplay between blockchains and contracting in organizations. Before discussing how blockchains may both substitute and complement contracts, we first elaborate on the role of contracts as important governance mechanisms.

### 4.1.1 Contracts as the Traditional Mechanism to Govern Collaboration

Relying on the legal system, contracts have become a common approach to organize collaborations. Contracts can be defined as legally enforceable agreements that contain obligations that are enforced or recognized by law (Poole, 2016). Contracts have been documented to be an effective approach to aligning interests between collaborating parties and organizing their intents into a legally binding agreement (Macneil, 1978; Reuer & Ariño, 2007; see Schepker et al., 2014 for a review). Contracts specify the rights and obligations of each party and provide clear payoff structures and sanctions (Parkhe, 1993; Zhou & Poppo, 2010). A contract can thus effectively protect the collaborating parties from the opportunistic behaviours of their partners (Schilke & Cook, 2015; Williamson, 1985).

In addition to facilitating cooperation, research has also documented contracts as an effective mechanism to facilitate coordination (Reuer & Ariño, 2007). Contracts can serve as a knowledge repository of a transaction (Mayer & Argyres, 2004), reminding the transacting parties of agreed-on aspects of the collaboration, such as the division of labour, task specification, and the roles and responsibilities of each party. A well-drafted contract can also generate a collaborative atmosphere by smoothing communication between parties (Malhotra & Lumineau, 2011; Mayer & Argyres, 2004). Transacting parties can thus use contracts to mitigate misunderstandings and reduce 'honest mistakes' (Mayer & Argyres, 2004), resulting in enhanced coordination outcomes.

In their role as a governance mechanism, contracts rely on legal enforceability. Under a legally binding contractual agreement, if a breach of contract occurs, the parties who signed the contract can pursue legal remedies, such as compensation or cancellation. Governmental bodies provide such power to ensure compliance to judicial verdicts. Therefore, a contract grants parties the right to find recourse to a court (or an arbitrator or mediator) to settle the dispute (Williamson, 1985). In this sense, whether a contract will be an effective governance mechanism depends heavily on the power of the legal system, which differs greatly across countries or even states (Oxley, 1999; Zhou & Xu, 2012).

### 4.1.2 Blockchains as an Alternative Way to Enforce Agreements

We suggest that blockchains can also serve the function of governing collaborations but in a way that is distinctive from legal contracts. Indeed, we see many partnership relations already being governed by blockchains. For example, AIG and Standard Chartered initiated a blockchain to improve efficiency in business-to-business multinational insurance policy offerings (IBM, 2021). Such transactions often involve multiple policies simultaneously and need to adhere to the regulations of multiple countries, which generates a large amount of information that needs to be consistent across different systems. Transparency and coordination between the insurance company and the protected clients are greatly needed. Blockchains provide a solution to issues in the insurance industry by enabling transparent and real-time information sharing, which significantly reduces the need for the reconciliation of records. Blockchains also automate policy payment and notification allocation (e.g., receipt) to participants through smart contracts, which minimizes human errors and fraud and boosts settlement speed. Another example comes from Microsoft, which has built a blockchain solution for the Xbox platform to achieve real-time royalty calculation and automatic payment for its partners, such as game developers, artists, and musicians (Arrowsmith, 2021).

Unlike contracts that depend on the legal system to enforce agreements, blockchains rely on algorithms to automatically enforce agreements. Protocols are written in the form of codes, specifying 'the rules for the distributed ledger; participation and validation; native digital assets; cryptograph; consensus (to make sure everyone has the identical copy of the ledger); and smart contracts' (Lacity, 2020, p. 117). With the establishment of protocols, the participating parties' actions must respect the rules.

Smart contracts play a central role in supporting the automatic enforcement of agreements on blockchains. Through interfaces called oracles, smart contracts monitor relevant information that is either native to blockchains or comes from the external environment (Hertig, 2020). Once the conditions that have been set earlier and are written into the code are satisfied, the agreements stored in these smart contracts will be executed automatically (see the DL Freight case as an illustration). Although they play an important role in the application of blockchains, the term 'smart contract' is somewhat of a misnomer (Durovic & Janssen, 2019). Despite what its name suggests, a smart contract is not truly a contract in the traditional sense because it enforces agreements through not the law but, rather, codes and algorithms. Nor is it smart because without going beyond the rules, it only faithfully runs what has been set by humans.

Relatedly and importantly, blockchains are not merely a digital version of contracting. Consider contracting practices realized through electronic data interchange (EDI), understood as 'standardized interorganizational communication between independent computerized information systems and associated technological components' (Damsgaard & Lyytinen, 1998, p. 276). EDI enables computers to share digital documents in a common electronic format, which lowers costs and increases the speed of information processing. Transacting parties have long used EDI to send and receive digital contracts, such as purchase orders (Clemons et al., 1993; Emmelhainz, 1988). However, these digital contracts are still traditional contracts in that they rely on the legal system to claim remedies if things go wrong. This process is fundamentally different from that in blockchains, which leverage codes and algorithms to enforce agreements.

The self-contained and autonomous system of formal rules reflected in the set of protocols in blockchains presents an alternative way of governing collaborations. This method does not depend directly on the external enforceability of the court system (Werbach, 2018). As such, blockchains 'create order without law and implement what can be thought of as private regulatory frameworks' (De Filippi & Wright, 2018, p. 5). Indeed, with regard to both cooperation and coordination, blockchains afford a qualitatively different approach to governance.

Blockchains thus facilitate cooperation by preventing opportunism from the beginning. Specifically, any behaviours that are inconsistent with the rules will not be acknowledged and executed. Fraudulent attempts to unilaterally change the records in blockchain systems will be rejected because these attempts do not abide by the consensus protocol. Failures of processing the payments after a partner completes their obligations will be eliminated because the smart contract will automatically execute the agreements upon detecting and verifying successful completion. In such a governance system, machines have deliberately been put on centre stage, while human intervention stays on the periphery.

Blockchains facilitate coordination through several mechanisms. Blockchains help provide participating parties with transparent information in a nearly real-time manner (Hanisch et al., 2022). Importantly, this information is verified so that misunderstandings can be greatly reduced. In addition, the protocols and codes are open-sourced so that the participants can have a consistent understanding of the rules by which the system works. This feature greatly enhances accountability (by defining roles and responsibilities for each node), predictability (by making sure tasks are performed in a planned manner), and common understanding (by aligning the knowledge and expectation of different parties), which are recognized as the three fundamental pillars constituting effective coordination (Okhuysen & Bechky, 2009).

### 4.1.3 Implications for Traditional Contracting: Substitutive and Complementary Effects

Because blockchains constitute an alternative governance mechanism, they may have significant implications for contracting. Given that blockchains do not directly rely on the legal system, they have the potential to act as *substitutes* for traditional contracting, which relies on the court's judicial function. Such substitution can lead to lower costs in certain types of transactions and certain collaboration stages since blockchains can fulfil most of the cooperation and coordination functions of traditional contracts but in a faster and less expensive way.

One implication of such a substitutive effect is that it allows blockchains to overcome some traditional contracting problems. Contracts are effective governance mechanisms only in situations when disputes can be reliably solved by judicial systems (Zhou & Poppo, 2010). However, in certain economies, contract enforcement can either be unreliable or require a substantial amount of time (Parmigiani & Rivera-Santos, 2015). In addition to being costly and time consuming, litigation processes may also damage firms' reputation (Pinkham & Peng, 2017). The lack of effective contract enforcing mechanisms thus results in the poor safeguarding of business assets, such as property rights, which can have dramatic consequences for many organizations.

In contrast, with blockchains and smart contracts governing transactions, these transactions can be executed and enforced in a self-contained system. Hence, the effectiveness of legal institutions becomes less critical. Blockchains may thus help circumvent the voids of legal enforceability in certain economies. At a broader level, blockchains can essentially govern transactions despite an absence of mature institutions. For example, in many areas of the world, economies are not supported by strong and reliable financial institutions, such as banks or credit unions. A large number of citizens are still underbanked. Blockchains can act as substitutes for the traditional centralized banking system by building a reliable financial infrastructure (IBM, 2020; New York Times, 2021).

Apart from potentially substituting for legal contracting, blockchains' unique features also make them a useful instrument for augmenting the merits of traditional contracting, suggesting a *complementary* effect. One way in which blockchains complement traditional contracting is through decreased information asymmetry. Blockchains provide immutable and tamperproof transactional records, which could be used as evidence to support more effective dispute settlements through judicial systems. As such, blockchains not only help overcome contracting voids in underdeveloped economies but are also useful in mature institutional environments. Moreover, by enabling enhanced transparency and maintaining a full history of records, blockchains make opportunistic behaviours more easily detectable. In this sense, blockchains magnify the effectiveness of the contracts' legal enforceability by making hidden misbehaviours observable. Blockchains can thus help maintain a fair, open, and honest collaborative environment. For example, with the procurement blockchain deployed by the U.S. General Services Administration (GSA), both vendors and the government are better off (Nayak & Nguyen, 2018). The government can realize a higher level of openness and fairness, which is desired by the public, while vendors can perceive that their transactions with the governmental agency are more effectively protected.

## 4.2 Blockchains and Trust

Trust is another fundamental element that is at the heart of collaboration. Trust can be defined as 'the willingness of a party to be vulnerable to the actions of another party' (Mayer et al., 1995, p. 712). Management scholars have put much effort into understanding the forms, antecedents, and consequences of trust at both the individual and organizational levels (Fulmer & Gelfand, 2012).

Although sometimes conflated with adjacent constructs, such as confidence and predictability, trust is conceptually distinct from them. Vulnerability and risk-taking are the key components of trust, distinguishing it from other constructs. As Mayer and colleagues (1995, p. 714) put it, 'in [trust] risk must be recognized and assumed, and such is not the case with confidence'. Control is another concept that is often discussed alongside trust (e.g., Cao & Lumineau, 2015; Long & Sitkin, 2018). According to agency theory, principals use control mechanisms (e.g., monitoring and incentives) to constrain agents' behaviours, align interests, and reduce risks. Scholars have viewed trust and control as parallel mechanisms that can generate confidence in a partner's behaviour and facilitate cooperation in the relationship (e.g., Das & Teng, 1998; Long & Weibel, 2018).

Blockchains can have a significant impact on trust among organizational actors. Interestingly, the nature of blockchains' impact on trust is far from consensual. Some propose that blockchains may crowd out trust for good and describe blockchains as trustless or trust-free systems (e.g., Bahga & Madisetti, 2016; Jaoude & Saade, 2019; Xia et al., 2017; Xu et al., 2019). In other words, participants in blockchains are argued to have no need to trust each other. Others, however, suggest that blockchains actually support trust in the network (e.g., Casey & Vigna, 2018; Shackelford & Myers, 2017). According to this view and as described in *The Economist* (2015), the promise of blockchains strongly relies on their role as a 'trust machine'.

Our own viewpoint is that blockchains neither eliminate nor create but rather effectively change several fundamental facets of trust. We see two major shifts in trust resulting from blockchains: what trust is (form of trust) and who needs to be trusted (targets of trust).

### 4.2.1 Change in the Form of Trust

Traditionally, collaborating parties make trustworthiness assessments based on their knowledge of the partner (Schilke et al., 2021). One central way of doing so is through prior relationships with the partner, in which parties develop a mutual understanding of their behavioural patterns. In turn, based on prior interactions, parties try to predict a partner's future behaviours and make corresponding decisions on whether to put themselves in a vulnerable position at the hands of this partner. Alternatively, when they do not have any prior relationships with the partner, collaborators can make trustworthiness judgements through reputation cues. Given the information asymmetry between strangers, reputation is an effective mechanism to signal trustworthiness and build initial trust beliefs (Koufaris & Hampton-Sosa, 2004).

In any of the above cases, the collaborating parties' identities matter greatly. In traditional scenarios, the parties' identities serve as critical reference points to build expectations about the partners' behaviours (Schilke & Cook, 2013). In other words, people trust others because of who they are. Moreover, human agents transact with each other directly, calling for a type of trust that is inherently relational and interpersonal.

Blockchains change this fundamental basis for trust. Specifically, instead of allowing human agents to interact with each other directly, blockchains enable technology to intermediate these relationships. Due to their decentralized design, blockchain systems do not require direct relationships between collaborators. In many public blockchains, participants do not even know with whom they are collaborating. However, what has not changed is that participants still need to build confidence that their partners will behave in a way that does not harm their interests, such that they will feel comfortable committing to the relationship.

Despite the lack of relational information needed to make trustworthiness judgements, the participants in a blockchain network still have good reason to believe that they are not receiving fraudulent information and that the recorded data have been verified and cannot be secretively erased or falsified. Smart contracts keep regulating the behaviours of human agents. The participants have good confidence that as soon as they fulfil their obligations, their partners will do their part based on what has been agreed upon. In other words, confidence is not generated through trust but through the blockchain's control function, which constrains actors' behaviours by rejecting deviant actions and allowing only acceptable ones. In this sense, instead of a trust machine, blockchains can be more accurately described as a confidence machine (De Filippi et al., 2020).

However, this is not to say that trust is no longer important in the context of blockchains. Following Luhmann (1979) and Lewis and Weigert (1985), we distinguish between personal trust and system trust. A system broadly refers to any impersonal structure that mediates the transactional relationships between actors (Pennington et al., 2003). In system-based trust, the importance of identity is marginalized. Faith in the integrity of the partner's behaviour is now backed by technology and algorithms that ensure the integrity of the whole system. As long as the system is functioning well, participants have confidence in the integrity of their partners. In this sense, the agency of human actors is replaced by technological processes, with the decision of whether and whom to trust falling to the system's competence. Instead of being vulnerable to the integrity, competence, and benevolence of individuals, actors now need to trust the reliability, functionality, and usefulness of the system (McKnight et al., 2011).

Based on this terminology, our main argument is that in exchanges facilitated by blockchains, the primary form of trust transforms from personal trust to system trust. When supported by codes and algorithms, people tend to decide that the benefits of making investments through technology exceed the risks of losing assets. This reasoning explains why in a decentralized system where no central parties run the network, people would choose to use their money to purchase cryptocurrencies, such as Bitcoin, from strangers, whose characteristics are unknown and with whom they do not have prior relationships or clear future collaboration prospects. People's confidence in positive exchange outcomes derives from their trust in the technological system.

### 4.2.2 Change in the Target of Trust

Despite the fact that blockchains aim to mitigate human interference and create system trust, there are still important human actors who play significant roles in creating trust. As Lewis and Weigert (1985, p. 983) note, 'System trust ultimately depends on personal trust'. The vulnerability of participants in the blockchain system depends ultimately on their behaviours. However, these individual trustees are no longer the counterparties in the transaction but, rather, other entities in the system. We suggest that in blockchains, the target of interpersonal trust include two sets of individuals: those who design the system and those who provide information feeds for the algorithms.

The trustworthiness of the blockchain system rests first on the trustworthiness of its developers. Machines follow only the orders programmed by developers. Thus, the backbone of system trust in blockchains is ultimately the reliability of the codes and algorithms. For this reason, system users need to trust developers in terms of both competence and goodwill. Although blockchains should ideally be designed to be immutable and resilient to malicious attacks, we should also consider the cognitive limitations of the developers. Some unintended, difficult-to-notice loopholes in the system might cause severe damage to the integrity of its functionality (Niranjanamurthy et al., 2019). At the same time, users need to be alert to ill-willed behaviours by developers. Intentional wrongdoings by developers, such as when developers put deliberate twists into the software for their own personal benefit, have been found to be a critical issue jeopardizing the effectiveness of software.

A second target of trust that becomes more important in blockchain systems are the entities providing information feeds for the algorithms. Some blockchains need only native information (that is, information attached to the blockchain) to run. Bitcoin is such an example since all information required to make Bitcoin transactions is located on-chain. However, for other blockchains, the effectiveness of organizing transactions depends on the quality of the information about the state of the world that is fed into algorithms (Halaburda, 2018). For example, if a smart contract needs to confirm the weather of a specific location to decide whether to execute a program, then real-time reliable information about the temperature and humidity is critical to execute this transaction. Such issues of incorrect or poor-quality input producing faulty output are also known as 'garbage in, garbage out' problems. As such, whether the entities providing the relevant information can be trusted is an important assessment that must be made by the system participants.

## 4.3 Blockchains and Organizational Design

Blockchains have the potential to greatly alter the organizational structure, perhaps most notably, by driving the decentralization of organizations. At the extreme, blockchains may even serve as the backbone of a new form of organizing – i.e., DAOs, which lack any hierarchal structure. To appreciate the implications of blockchains in terms of organizational design, we briefly revisit the definition of organizations, the key challenges of organizing, and traditional organizational forms.

### 4.3.1 Organization, Organizing, and Traditional Organizational Forms

Four common components underlie the various conceptualizations of what an organization is. An organization is '(1) a multiagent system with (2) identifiable boundaries and (3) system-level goals (purpose) towards which (4) the constituent agent's efforts are expected to make a contribution' (Puranam et al., 2014, p. 165). Universal organizing issues include task division, task allocation, provision of rewards, and provision of information (Puranam, 2018). New organizational forms have the potential to change one or more of these four organizing issues.

Traditionally, organizations are governed by strict hierarchies. Organizations are usually understood as bureaucratic models, with managers controlling information and making decisions. This view was most clearly reflected in Taylorism (also known as scientific management) at the end of the nineteenth century. More than a century later, despite key innovations in organizational structures, including functional, multidivisional, and matrix structures, the hierarchical relationships between managers and employees are still the backbone of the information flow and decision rights of organizations.

Such traditional hierarchical structures have both advantages and disadvantages (Williamson, 1975). They can support efficient decision-making by helping to integrate information through clear lines of authority and reporting. They can also provide a clear understanding of employee roles and responsibilities as well as accountability for actions at different management levels. However, these hierarchy-based structures can involve complicated chains of command that can slow decision-making. Therefore, they come with the disadvantage of low flexibility to adapt and to react to unforeseen environmental and market pressures (Volberda, 1996). Moreover, in these organizational structures, a lack of autonomy can cause a strain on employee–manager relationships and create a disconnect between employees from top-level management.

### 4.3.2 Towards More Decentralized Organizations?

Blockchains can introduce a departure from these traditional hierarchy-based forms of an organization. In particular, blockchains enable the rise of a new organizational form called DAOs. DAOs can be defined as 'non-hierarchical organizations that perform and record routine tasks on a peer-to-peer, cryptographically secure, public network, and rely on the voluntary contributions of their internal stakeholders to operate, manage, and evolve the organization through a democratic consultation process' (Hsieh et al., 2018, p. 2). Unlike traditional organizational forms, in a DAO, there are no managers or owners. People work with peers following transparent rules contained in codes and algorithms. DAOs use tokens to incentivize participants to do their jobs, such as validating information. Smart contracts are often critical to the operation of DAOs because they automate activities, such as rewarding participants once they successfully complete a given task. DAOs use algorithms and codes to perform organizational routines and rely on democratic votes to alter those routines.

The first real-world implementation of a DAO was Bitcoin (Hsieh et al., 2018). Bitcoin's objective, similar to that of a bank, is to provide a payment system. However, unlike a bank with headquarters, subsidiaries, managers, and employees, Bitcoin consists solely of a network of users and miners who have no hierarchical power over each other (Antonopoulos, 2014). Bitcoin uses PoW as the consensus mechanism, which requires miners to compete with each other in solving complex mathematical puzzles. Since each puzzle can be resolved only by random guesses, the probability of successfully solving the puzzle is proportional to the miner's computing power (Garay et al., 2015). The node that solves the puzzle first obtains the right to add new blocks. As such, decisions are made following collective voting processes based on the computation powers of miners, which may vary due to the hardware employed (e.g., processing speed of the chips). The whole organization runs in adherence to the Bitcoin protocols, which are made transparent as open-source codes.

To better understand how DAOs differ from traditional organizations in addressing the fundamental tasks of organizing, Hsieh and colleagues' (2018) illustration of the differences between Bitcoin and banks provides a useful starting point. First, while traditional banks centralize task division top-down, in Bitcoin, task division is based on the computing power of miners. Thus, where tasks are traditionally allocated by managers, in Bitcoin, miners self-select into the network. Second, reward schemes are usually kept private in traditional banks. In contrast, in Bitcoin, the compensation for miners is automated, randomized, and fully transparent. Third, traditional banks centrally control information, while in Bitcoin, historical information is kept transparent, and all participants have the same version of the truth.

Beyond payment systems, another well-known DAO is the distributed venture capital fund on Ethereum, also known as The DAO (or Ð). Despite being short-lived due to a notorious attack (which we will return to later), The DAO has received considerable attention as an important experiment in implementing a DAO that allocates resources in a distributed and decentralized fashion. The DAO functioned very much akin to a venture capital fund but operated in a completely different, decentralized way (DuPont, 2017). Namely, investors made the decisions directly rather than fund managers. They voted for the entrepreneurial proposals using their tokens (i.e., ethers on the Ethereum blockchain). Since tokens are valuable, voting for a proposal virtually means funding it. Subsequent decisions – from the hiring of a particular employee of the entrepreneurial start-up to eventual pay-outs to investors – were also made automatically through smart contracts based on the votes and the performance of the projects. Thus, as an organization that serves a specific objective, The DAO did not involve hierarchical chains in decision-making processes. Smart contracts and tokens together powered the operation of the organization. Similarly structured DAOs that were established more recently include Dash, a cryptocurrency that is governed through decentralized voting on proposals for improving the ecosystem, and MakerDAO, which also relies on decentralized voting on changes to key parameters in smart contracts to keep the value of Dai (a cryptocurrency) stable.

All these examples show how algorithms can replace human actors in coordinating certain organizational activities and integrating everyone's efforts without human actors giving orders (Murray et al., 2021b). Therefore, although DAOs fall well into the definition of organizations, this new organizational form challenges many assumptions commonly seen in traditional organizational research; thus, traditional organizational theories may not apply. Since formal managers do not exist in DAOs, fiat and authority are no longer the 'signature' of internal organizing (Williamson, 1996). Principal–agent problems that are pervasive in traditional organizations are eliminated or greatly reduced. While DAOs do not assume agency problems away, they leverage algorithms and computational power to circumvent them.

Despite powering a new decentralized organizational form, i.e., DAOs, blockchains may benefit organizations by solving certain organizational problems, reducing costs, and building trust within traditional organizations (PwC, 2020). A recent report by the Committee of Sponsoring Organizations of the Treadway Commission (COSO) explains how to use blockchains to consolidate internal control, for example, control with regard to financial reporting. They contend that blockchains can 'help facilitate an effective control environment (e.g., by recording transactions with minimal human intervention)' (Burns et al., 2020, p. 2).

To understand how blockchains may benefit internal organizing, Murray and colleagues' (2021a) analysis shows that blockchains can help reduce certain types of agency costs by allowing the removal of certain agent managers, as illustrated in DAOs. As such, blockchains greatly reduce the need (and thus the cost) of monitoring the agents' motivations. In addition, information asymmetries make it necessary for principals to devote considerable efforts to monitoring the organization's operations (e.g., supply chain management). Blockchains can help overcome such information asymmetries by maintaining verified and shared information. False claims of facts by managers can be reduced, which frees organizations from costly third-party auditing and verification. All of these effects imply that blockchains can save the agency costs that would be incurred without proper governance and that are due to agents' self-serving behaviours.

In this section, we discussed how blockchains enable more decentralized organizational forms and how DAOs, as extreme versions of decentralized organizations, may circumvent significant costs. In terms of solving the four universal issues of organizing, Table 6 summarizes the major differences between traditional centralized organizational forms and blockchain-based decentralized forms (Puranam, 2018). However, despite the benefits of reducing costs, our view is that DAOs will ultimately not crowd out all traditional organizations. Organizations exist for reasons other than minimizing cost, e.g., pooling resources, consolidating power, and sharing identity (Santos & Eisenhardt, 2005). In addition, blockchains can ease the processes of agreement execution and monitoring but appear less adequate for other tasks requiring more creativity, such as the identification of opportunities and the creation and maintenance of organizational values (inspiration, purpose, vision, leadership; Selznick, 1957). It will be exciting to follow the future evolution of DAOs and to see to what extent they eventually replace or complement traditional organizational forms.

## 5 Critiques and Pitfalls

Although blockchains offer many advantages, there are also important challenges and pitfalls of which managers and organizations should be aware.

**Table 6** A comparison between traditional centralized and blockchain-enabled decentralized organizational forms

| Universal problems of organizing | Traditional centralized forms of organization | Blockchain-enabled decentralized organization |
| --- | --- | --- |
| Task division | Organization designers decide on the task structure, encoded in documentations such as the charter | Organization designers decide the task structure, encoded in codes and algorithms by developers |
| Task allocation | Managers match tasks with subordinates based on skill sets | Members self-select into tasks |
| Reward distribution | Rewards are defined by compensation policies and determined by an authoritative superior | Rewards are defined by the blockchain protocol and determined automatically based on the specific consensus mechanism |
| Information flow | Information flows along hierarchies and is concentrated in top management | Information flows directly between members in a decentralized way |

In this section, we introduce several critical points that should be considered in the process of technology adoption and diffusion.

## 5.1 Risks of System Failure

Any IT system is subject to possible failure, such as hacks of large databases or malfunctions of the national electricity grid. The larger the system is, the more severe the consequences. The SWIFT network hack on 12 January 2015 illustrates this issue; unidentified hackers stole $12 million from transactions between Wells Fargo and Banco del Austro (BDA) (Bergin & Layne, 2015).

Compared to other IT systems, blockchains are known to be difficult to break. The first and largest blockchain, the Bitcoin blockchain, has not had severe protocol issues since it was launched in 2009, despite some fraud and hacks at the application level (e.g., Bitcoin wallets). However, such a high level of security and reliability cannot be taken for granted. Even though blockchains are meant to be unbreakable, some unexpected holes in the codes can have potentially disastrous consequences for the whole network if the system breaks down. In 2016, an unknown hacker exploited a loophole in the smart contracts of The DAO, which was built on the Ethereum blockchain. The hacker successfully drained more than 3.6 million ethers, equivalent to approximately US$50 million at the time. Although the hack did not break the Ethereum protocol, The DAO represented a large application on the Ethereum blockchain, and the hack 'almost brought Ethereum down' (Leising, 2017).

The advancement of quantum computing also poses a security threat to blockchains. Quantum computing offers a new way of solving computational problems by leveraging theories of quantum mechanisms (Knill, 2010). The devices that can perform such computational tasks, called quantum computers, can substantially outperform traditional computers in certain types of computing tasks (e.g., finding the prime factors of an integer). This new type of computation is likely to revolutionize cryptography and therefore jeopardize the effectiveness of blockchain technology. Quantum computers are believed to acquire the ability in the future to attack key technological processes that blockchain systems rely on, such as digital signatures and cryptographic hash functions (Kiktenko et al., 2018). As such, scholars and developers have been working on designing so-called post-quantum blockchains that are resistant to quantum computing attacks (Fernandez-Carames & Fraga-Lamas, 2020).

In the face of a system breakdown, centralized systems may prove more resilient in many ways than decentralized systems. In centralized systems, there are clear targets of responsibility. The centralized owners of systems, such as the bank of a financial system or Facebook of its social network, are accountable for system maintenance and resolution. In addition, centralized systems can be more efficient in terms of crisis decision-making and coordination than decentralized systems. As such, actions in response to a system failure might be implemented comparatively faster in centralized systems.

In contrast, for decentralized systems such as blockchains, it can be more difficult to fix such problems. Since there is no system owner, there is no clear locus of accountability when disruptions occur. To make things even more challenging, it can be difficult to repair broken blockchain systems since they are deliberately designed to be very costly to change. Rigidity and inflexibility are merits of blockchains in stable environments, yet when disruptions occur, these features become critical liabilities.

In the 2016 Ethereum hack, when the community realized that the event had occurred, the only way to correct things was to have at least 51 per cent of all nodes agree and vote on a corrective strategy. Ironically, the PoW system was initially designed to ensure that no one had enough power to rewrite history. Ultimately, Vitalik Buterin, cofounder of Ethereum, mobilized most participants of the Ethereum community to form a 'hard fork', which is essentially a different version of the blockchain that runs in parallel to the original. This event generated ethical debates since the hacker actually operated within the rules. Interestingly, the original blockchain is still running today because some proponents believe that it is the real blockchain and that the hard fork is a counterfeit and should not have been created. Such a series of events undermined the image of blockchain technology, showing that it is not truly immutable because once someone accumulates 51 per cent of the voting rights (which happened in the Ethereum case), the transactions that had already occurred could be nullified, which of course undermines the very purpose of blockchains.

In summary, the risk of system failure in blockchains, however small, does exist. Once bad things happen in such systems, it can be very costly to correct them.

## 5.2 Technological Limitations

Blockchain technology is in its infancy, and it is thus not surprising that several technological challenges still need to be addressed, including the *oracle problem*, *environmental issues*, and *confidentiality*.

A blockchain oracle is a third-party service that provides information for smart contracts that is external to the blockchain. A prerequisite for the effective execution of smart contracts is to ensure that the information feeds are reliable and trustworthy. After all, blockchains are technologies used for storing information, not acquiring it. Their usefulness thus depends on the quality of their information feeds. However, information providers might be subject to dishonest behaviours or malicious attacks, which are sometimes referred to as the *oracle problem*.

The oracle problem calls for caution regarding the interface between blockchains and the physical world. Similar issues occur with applications that are built upon the blockchain protocol – for example, the Bitcoin wallet applications connecting the blockchain and users. While the Bitcoin blockchain itself may be difficult to hack, hackers have attacked its wallet application and stolen users' personal information, including email addresses, full names, phone numbers, and postal addresses (Bambrough, 2020). Therefore, vulnerabilities at the interface between the blockchain and the real world remain major challenges.

Another issue is the *consumption of significant resources* to execute blockchains. Specifically, to operate blockchains based on the PoW consensus (e.g., Bitcoin and Ethereum), the nodes that are responsible for verification (called miners) must compete with each other in solving mathematical puzzles, which consumes a large amount of electricity. According to recent reports, the electricity consumed annually to mine Bitcoins has exceeded the electricity consumption of some nation states, such as Argentina (Aratani, 2021; Criddle, 2021).

However, with advancements in technologies and the evolution of generations of blockchains, energy consumption is becoming a less critical issue (even though it is nonetheless a real concern for the two largest blockchains). Practitioners are actively looking for solutions to reduce energy consumption. A case in point is the EZ blockchain, which develops a solution that utilizes natural gas flaring waste from drilling and refining for industrial crypto mining. Another case is SolarCoin, which links the reward of cryptocurrencies with the supply of solar energy to incentivize more ecological accomplishments (Dierksmeier & Seele, 2018).

Other consensus mechanisms do not link voting power with the consumption of scarce resources. The aforementioned PoS is one example. Accordingly, in its upgrade plan, Ethereum has been working on changing its consensus mechanism from PoW to PoS (Ethereum, 2021). Others include proof-of-authority, proof-of-elapsed-time, and practical Byzantine fault tolerance (see Table 2). Although these consensus mechanisms circumvent the severe problem of energy consumption, they also afford relatively less assurance of system security.

Finally, *confidentiality* is another key concern. At best, blockchains provide pseudonymity (Nakamoto, 2008), which is a weaker form of anonymity. It is possible to use supervised machine learning to predict the unidentified entities in the Bitcoin system (Yin et al., 2019). Moreover, organizations usually do not want everyone in the network to be able to review their information – they only want certain actors to view certain information. Such privacy concerns constitute one of the major hurdles preventing enterprises from adopting blockchain technologies (Lacity, 2020). Considerable effort has been devoted to solving the privacy issues with public blockchains, for example, by developing solutions to hide the details of transactions between wallets (Duncan, 2019).

## 5.3 Challenges to Full Decentralization

Another critique of blockchains is that full decentralization may be illusive, at least in the current stage of technology development. In addition to technological challenges, many human factors or biases – such as hubris, overconfidence in making the best decisions, and the desire to control and obtain personal power – will pose limits to the full decentralization of blockchains. A considerable level of concentration of voting power may lead to possible attacks on the system, such as attempting to change the shared record without obtaining consensus from others. Such attacks damage the promised security and immutability of the recorded information on blockchains.

In practice, many factors can lead certain actors to have disproportionate voting power in a blockchain, leading to increased centralization. Since computational power is particularly important in the mining competition on PoW blockchains, a joint group of miners may pool together large amounts of computational power to leverage economies of scale, forming what has been called mining pools. This arrangement poses the risk of overconcentrated power on blockchains that use PoW consensus mechanisms. According to data from btc.com (https://btc.com/stats/pool), as of 29 April 2021, the four largest Bitcoin mining pools accounted for approximately 15.8 per cent, 15.6 per cent, 11.6 per cent, and 10.9 per cent of the voting power. Collusion thus becomes much easier since, together, these pools control over 51 per cent of the voting power. In a smaller public blockchain based on PoW consensus mechanisms, it is even easier for a single entity to gain 51 per cent of the voting power to mount a direct attack on the system by creating fraudulent blocks and deceiving the other users.

Other types of blockchain systems also face the issue of power concentration. In PoS blockchains, mining power is distributed on the basis of the proportion of coins held by a miner, meaning that entities that hold a large share of coins in the system will have more concentrated voting power. Once they obtain 51 per cent of all stakes, they have the power to perform a 51 per cent attack. Compared to PoW, the PoS mechanism leverages a different logic of ensuring that the attack is unlikely to happen. Since the miners with higher voting power also have more stakes, protecting the integrity of the system is actually in their best interest.

For many permissioned blockchains, such as the IBM HyperLedger, the founders or founding consortia retain a considerable amount of power in the network. For example, they have the power to grant access control and upgrade protocols (Carson et al., 2018). Even though it is often easier to start a blockchain project led by a founder or a founding consortium, it is critical for founding teams of permissioned blockchains to relinquish power so that others can be convinced to join the system and realize the full promise of blockchains (Sternberg et al., 2021).

As such, in the current stage of development, decentralization is better understood as a gradual concept. Indeed, blockchains differ along a continuum of different decentralization levels, which vary depending on several factors, such as the adopted consensus algorithm and the number of participants in the network (Werbach, 2018). It is also useful to distinguish decentralization across different stages of activities in terms of blockchain adoption, including initial system development, subsequent system updates, transaction validation, and transactions (Halaburda & Mueller-Bloch, 2020).

Different levels of decentralization are motivated by trade-offs in blockchain design. Although fully decentralized blockchains have appealing levels of security and immutability, they are often lacking in terms of other aspects, including scalability and privacy. These features, which we will elaborate in the next section, are oftentimes particularly valued by enterprises seeking blockchain solutions. For this reason, the governance *of* blockchain systems may require both on- and off-chain governance efforts (i.e., decision-making that occurs outside the blockchain and away from the code base) to ensure system effectiveness.

## 5.4 The Regulation Paradox and Ethical Issues

The issue of blockchain regulation poses an intriguing dilemma. On the one hand, blockchains were initially designed to eliminate centralized control and oversight. By introducing regulation, the technology may lose some of its most attractive features, such as decentralization and censor resistance.

On the other hand, without proper regulation, blockchains may pose a threat to public welfare. Due to the ease of transfer and the pseudonymity of cryptocurrencies, blockchains have created hotbeds for criminal activity, such as money laundering and terrorist financing (Rooney, 2021). Dierksmeier and Seele (2020) provide several illustrations of blockchain-induced criminal activities. For example, blockchains have induced a new form of online crime called 'cryptojacking', which incentivizes people to hack into high-performance computers for their own mining purposes. Another recent example is the extortion targeting Colonial Pipeline by the ransomware extortionists Darkside, which involved the payment of 63.7 Bitcoins (equivalent to US\$2.3 million) as ransom (U.S. Department of Justice, 2021).

Moreover, compared to centralized systems, blockchains can be less resilient in terms of unexpected shocks. The negative outcomes induced by these shocks are directly borne by users. For example, when the attack on The DAO occurred in 2016, the community could do little to stop the attack, and the losses of users' ethers could not be recovered. Proper regulations will be necessary in protecting users' interests (Leonard, 2019). In addition, since blockchains themselves have no capacity to guarantee the authenticity of offline data, supervision by the law is still needed to regulate improper behaviours (Chang et al., 2020a).

Therefore, while many governments are pondering their own national blockchain strategy (e.g., Schallbruch & Skierka, 2018), they have also noticed the potential negative effects that can arise from the use of blockchains. For example, Australia, the United States, China, Switzerland, and the UK have enacted regulations regarding the use of blockchains and cryptocurrencies. However, similar to regulating any emerging technology, regulating blockchains is difficult and requires that regulators understand the technology and its impact on the economy across sectors (Swanson, 2020). At least thus far, governments' efforts to create and impose adequate regulations are generally lagging behind blockchain development (Lee & Shin, 2018).

Such efforts require active collaboration between the government and entrepreneurs. For example, LO3 Energy, an energy company providing blockchain-powered service to facilitate decentralized energy exchange between neighbourhoods, has been working closely with New York regulators and policymakers to help them understand relevant concepts and processes. Companies' proactive collaboration with governments can constitute a vital step to ensure the implementation of favourable policies.

In blockchain adoption, important ethical challenges that extend beyond legal aspects also deserve consideration. Since blockchains enable the replication of the whole history of records, every user on a blockchain faces the risk of owning unsolicited, arbitrary content. This feature may cause unwanted trouble, such as unintended violations of copyrights, downloading of malware, and accidentally obtaining politically sensitive or even illegal content (Matzutt et al., 2018).

However, it is equally important to note that blockchains can support ethical behaviours. The transparency and traceability of the information rendered by blockchains facilitate fairness and authenticity, which can help combat unethical behaviours in a broad range of domains – from supply chain quality management to governmental corruption. Furthermore, blockchains also help address ethical issues in artificial intelligence (AI). To develop fair and trustworthy AI, it is important to ensure data transparency during the AI training process. Blockchains can effectively deliver such requirements of input transparency (Bertino et al., 2019).

## 6 Conclusions and Implications

The ongoing discussion around the features, potential, and challenges of blockchains leads us to analyse their implications for both practitioners and researchers. Managers should consider blockchains as an important strategic tool to organize collaborations, in part replacing traditional contracts and social mechanisms. Additionally, they should consider the joint use of different approaches to mitigate collaborative hazards and enhance efficiency. Moreover, managers should be aware of both the benefits and costs of adopting blockchain technologies. Given their practical relevance, blockchains can provide rich opportunities for further scholarly enquiry into management. We propose a new framework to guide future research and to systematically develop a comprehensive understanding of this important phenomenon and its implications for management theory. We end this Element with a brief discussion of future blockchain possibilities.

## 6.1 Managerial Implications

### 6.1.1 A New Strategic Tool for Organizing Collaborations

One of the major managerial implications of blockchains is that they enrich managers' toolkit for organizing collaborations (Lumineau et al., 2021c). In addition to using traditional contracting and relational norms to address problems in partnerships, managers can now consider using blockchains to support their partnerships. We suggest that blockchains can fundamentally change all three phases of a collaboration: partner selection, agreement formation, and execution, as illustrated in Figure 3.

Regarding the selection of a good partner, managers usually rely on past experiences or public reputations to make decisions. However, when managers are collaborating with strangers for the first time, relevant trustworthiness cues are scarce and diffuse. In addition, small and young firms often lack a public reputation (Schilke et al., 2017). As previously noted, blockchains can greatly facilitate collaboration with strangers or parties with no reputation record. Blockchains also come with a deterrence effect, whereby dishonest or incompetent partners are likely to refrain from entering blockchains. Hence, blockchains can be a useful instrument for managers to broaden their search for potential partners and to increase the quality of partner selection.

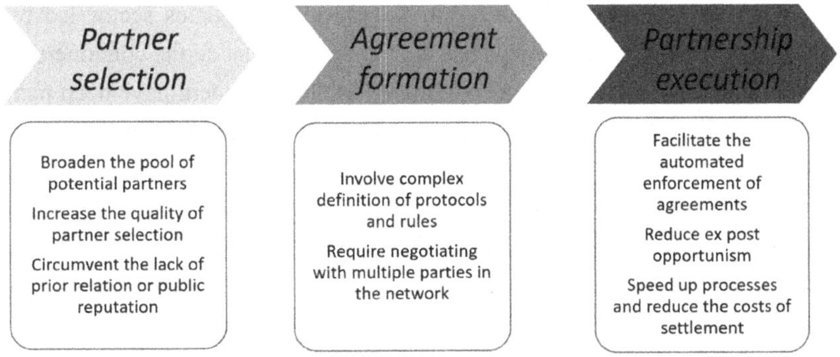

**Figure 3** How blockchains impact the different stages of collaboration

Managers need to be wary of possible pitfalls in the agreement formation phase when using blockchains. Due to the inherent inflexibility of the blockchain structure, the agreements reflected in the protocols and codes must be carefully defined *ex ante*. Negotiating the setup of the blockchain involves multiple parties in the network rather than a traditional two-party interaction, which explains why it can be costly and complicated to establish a permissioned blockchain within a consortium (Vigliotti & Jones, 2020). Regarding blockchain infrastructure, many important choices must be made and negotiated among consortium members, given that updating the protocols tends to be very costly.

In the execution stage, a significant benefit of using blockchains is that they facilitate the automated enforcement of agreements. Thus, there is less room for dishonest behaviours, and opportunism can be greatly reduced. In addition, since immutable records on blockchains can augment the effectiveness of traditional contracts, the use of blockchains adds an additional layer of protection for relationship-specific investments. Moreover, blockchains can speed up processes and reduce the cost of settlements by providing a single version of the truth for all participants, thus greatly enhancing efficiency in the execution stage of the collaboration.

### 6.1.2 When to Use Blockchains and When to Combine Them with Other Collaboration Approaches

Given the various challenges inherent to blockchains in their current stage of development, blockchains are clearly not a panacea for every situation. Their effectiveness depends on the particular context in which they are applied. Specifically, we suggest that blockchains can be most effective when an agreement can be written in clear computer language and when its outcomes are verifiable. An example in which such conditions are satisfied is the

TradeLens blockchain, an initiative in the maritime logistics sector led by Maersk and IBM. Smart contracts use the temperature inside the containers as a criterion to identify whether the conditions in the agreement have been met. In this case, the temperature is verifiable and can be objectively measured by sensors.

In contrast, for other collaborations in which key conditions cannot be easily assessed and verified, the use of blockchains alone is often not sufficient. For example, in many service transactions, such as those of legal consulting businesses, service quality is difficult to assess and formulate *ex ante* in clear computer language. Collaborating parties will likely have to rely on traditional legal contracts and social mechanisms to manage their relationships. These mechanisms are more open-ended and allow for human interpretation of the agreements, granting some flexibility to the agreement.

One implication for managers here is that in many circumstances, it will be most appropriate to consider the joint use of different approaches to govern collaborations (Lumineau et al., 2021b). Again taking the TradeLens case as an example, while collaborators can use blockchains to support the successful transportation and delivery of cargo, the carrier and cargo owner may still want to sign traditional legal contracts to stipulate the scope and boundaries of their collaboration. Managers thus need to carefully consider which activities of their partnership can indeed benefit from the deployment of blockchain technology and which parts are less likely to do so and, in turn, should still be governed by traditional methods.

### 6.1.3 Creating New Business Models

While improving the efficiency of managing existing operations, blockchains also create new opportunities for value creation and value capture (Malhotra et al., 2022). They enable the provision of products or services that were either not previously available or very difficult to realize. Some examples include widespread decentralized platforms supporting different types of activities, such as artwork investments (e.g., Artolin, Maecenas), music sharing and purchasing (e.g., Mediachain, Ujo), and online communities of original content (e.g., Steemit, Akasha). These platforms have no centralized owners coordinating and approving activities. Instead, the participants directly communicate with each other and democratically verify and record transactions. Such new business models are appealing not only because they are free of censorship but also because the transacting parties can capture more value since no third party to mediate the transactions is needed. Another example is blockchain-based solutions of cross-border financial settlements, such as payment (e.g., Ripple, Stella) or issuance of letters of credit (e.g., Standard Chartered, 2019). Such new solutions are both secure and fast, greatly eliminating the long settlement time of traditional money transfer and document processing (Fanning & Centers, 2016).

Opportunities abound for firms to offer blockchains as a service. Firms such as IBM, Microsoft, and R3 create value from building and promoting their own blockchain platform to offer infrastructure for others to develop customized applications. Other firms specialize in providing technical support for consulting services around blockchain technology (e.g., Ernst & Young, PwC). For example, Ernst & Young provides wide-ranging blockchain consulting services, ranging from blockchain opportunity assessment to planning, implementation, and integration into the existing organization and value chain.

### 6.1.4 The Blockchain Implementation Process

To reap the full benefits of blockchain technology, organizations must first develop a deep understanding of how blockchains may add value to their business by solving certain problems. In this regard, the blockchain cases included throughout this Element – from Maersk Tradelens to the Microsoft Xbox case – may serve as useful examples that showcase how blockchains can improve particular organizational processes.

Adopting blockchain technologies and capturing their benefits require organizations to develop a distinct set of skills. Since blockchains are based on machine language, nontechnical employees may find it challenging to understand the business logics in smart contracts. Therefore, in addition to legal personnel who oversee the use of traditional contracts, organizations should hire specialized computer scientists who can read and understand programming language in smart contracts. At the same time, computer professionals may not fully understand the business context and managerial requirements. Therefore, organizations need to develop superior capabilities to smoothen coordination between business personnel and technicians to fully integrate their efforts.

Beyond understanding the strategic implications of blockchains for their organizations, managers should also pay attention to some caveats and barriers to successful implementation of the technology. Malhotra and colleagues (2022) point to three sets of risks in implementing blockchains – technological risks, business risks, and legal risks. Technology-wise, as noted earlier in Section 5, blockchains still have significant room for improvement towards better security, privacy, and scalability. At the same time, adopting blockchains may require changes in the flow of operations and the business model of an organization. These changes may create internal dissonance and resistance from some organizational members. Finally, regulatory challenges are surely one of the major issues. As noted earlier, governments around the world are concerned about both the advantages and regulatory needs of blockchains. Managers should be aware of the regulatory uncertainties and ensure that blockchain implementation complies with legislation. Managers can also actively seek to work with the government to help it understand the phenomenon and practical issues, which will ultimately benefit the managers' own operations.

## 6.2 Implications for Scholars

### 6.2.1 An Agenda for Blockchain Governance Research

As indicated in our literature review, there are several approaches to studying blockchains. In this Element, we suggest that one particularly fruitful approach is to view blockchains as a new governance mechanism to organize collaborations. Blockchain governance employs codes and algorithms to enforce agreements, which is different than traditional contracting that relies on the legal system. We invite future scholars to adopt this perspective and to offer greater detail on the governance function of blockchains in a number of ways (see Table 7 for a summary of our suggestions).

The first step is to better depict relevant differences across blockchains. We need to better understand the critical dimensions along which blockchains differ. One broad distinction applied in prior research is between permissionless and permissioned blockchains, yet this coarse classification approach may overlook important nuances within each category. For example, we need to understand how to characterize different permissionless blockchains to build a more refined understanding of their respective governance features.

We also envision interesting avenues to explore the different control and coordination mechanisms of blockchain governance. This issue has been well documented in the contracting literature, where legal contracts have been found to facilitate control and coordination by specifying rights and obligations, penalties, conflict resolution rules, task divisions and roles, and contingency adaptations (Lumineau & Malhotra, 2011; Schepker et al., 2014). For blockchain governance, we see exciting opportunities for scholars to identify and operationalize relevant constructs to theoretically depict the degree of control and coordination in blockchain governance.

Relatedly, we see the boundary conditions of effective blockchain governance as constituting an important issue and promising research opportunity. Like other governance mechanisms, blockchain governance has both advantages and limitations; thus, we need to understand what kinds of transactions can – and cannot – be effectively governed by blockchains. Lumineau and colleagues (2021a) suggest that the tacitness of a transaction determines the

**Table 7** A summary of the research agenda

| Research fields | Relevant themes | Examples of research questions |
| --- | --- | --- |
| Blockchain governance | Characterizing blockchain governance | • What are the critical dimensions along which blockchains differ?<br>• How can we theoretically depict and empirically measure the degree of control and coordination in blockchain governance? |
| | Boundary conditions | • What types of transactions can be more efficiently governed through blockchains?<br>• What geographical and temporal factors impact the efficiency of blockchain governance? |
| | Interplay among governance mechanisms | • How does blockchain governance interact with other forms of governance?<br>• How should managers choose (combinations of) different forms of governance? |
| | Performance implication | • What performance indicators should be used to measure the efficiency and effectiveness of blockchain governance?<br>• Under what conditions can blockchains create competitive advantages for adopting organizations? |
| Blockchains and trust | Shift in the form of trust | • How do the trajectories of system trust in the context of blockchains change over time?<br>• What are the most effective trust repair processes after a breach of system trust?<br>• What are the sources of production of system trust?<br>• How can organizations build competitive advantages given the increasing importance of system trust? |

**Table 7** (cont.)

| Research fields | Relevant themes | Examples of research questions |
|---|---|---|
| | Shift in the target of trust | • How do people make judgements regarding the trustworthiness of those they do not know? |
| Blockchains and organizational design | Understanding DAOs | • How do the unique ways of organizing activities in a DAO impact collaborative dynamics and performance?<br>• How do DAOs differ from other forms of so-called decentralized organizations? |
| | Choosing from different organizational forms | • What are the trade-offs of choosing the different organizational forms?<br>• What kinds of tasks are most suitable to organize via DAOs? |
| | Strategic human resources | • How will the work of different types of managers be impacted?<br>• What types of skillsets will become the most valuable forms of strategic human capital? |

domain of effective blockchain governance. A transaction is said to be tacit (explicit) when the conditions are relatively difficult (easy) to codify and the outcomes are difficult (easy) to verify. Blockchains appear more useful in the context of more explicit transactions, whereas their value seems relatively lower whenever a transaction is difficult to codify and verify. Going beyond tacitness, an investigation of other potentially relevant characteristics of transactions (e.g., the degree of asset specificity, uncertainty, and frequency; the exchange of digital versus physical assets; or the distinction between bilateral versus multilateral ties) should be made to appreciate the precise conditions under which blockchains can create substantial value.

Relevant boundary conditions of effective blockchain governance may also involve geographical and temporal factors. A geographical area's technological maturity and diffusion of infrastructures (e.g., the Internet, smartphones, or computers) are likely to impact the viability of blockchain governance. At the same time, emerging economies might benefit more from blockchains than developed countries where institutions have already been well established.

Blockchains could be an effective alternative in countries in which legal institutions are weak and where enforcing legal contracts can be costly and uncertain (Cao et al., 2018). In addition, scholars could consider the timing of blockchain adoption for different organizations. The choice between building a blockchain or joining an existing initiative might depend on different strategic considerations. Scholars could also examine the trade-offs between moving early or at a later stage. An example is provided by Park and colleagues (2020), who show that despite the opportunity to raise funds by being an early mover in ICOs, these start-ups may face the risk of knowledge spillover that might be detrimental to the venture's future performance.

Furthermore, we need to better understand the interplay between blockchain governance and other governance mechanisms, such as traditional contracting. In this Element, we suggest that blockchains may both substitute and complement traditional contracting through different logics and under different conditions (see Section 4.1 for more details). Future research can empirically investigate our predictions about the joint use of different governance mechanisms. Such studies will provide valuable guidance for practitioners.

Finally, we need more empirical evidence to understand the performance implications of blockchain governance. Scholars first have to identify useful performance indicators – such as cost overruns, delays, quality control, or partner satisfaction – and observe changes in these indicators as a result of deploying blockchains. Strategy scholars should be particularly interested in understanding whether using blockchains can result in a competitive advantage. Any performance effects of blockchains are likely to be contingent on factors, such as the type of blockchain, the particular transaction, and other conditions, including geography and timing.

### 6.2.2 An Agenda for Blockchains and Trust Research

The shift from personal to system trust brings opportunities for scholars to re-examine trust dynamics, that is, the trajectories of trust development in the context of blockchains. For example, some scholars suggest that personal trust tends to be low in the beginning phase of a relationship (e.g., Zand, 1972). However, system-based trust, such as the trust enabled by blockchains, may follow a different path. Indeed, there is initial evidence that trust in technological systems tends to be relatively high in the adoption phase but then gradually decreases over time as it diffuses (Glikson & Woolley, 2020). Potential overtrust in a system may lead to detrimental results, as illustrated by the high percentage of ICO scams to which people fall victim (Alexandre, 2018).

The shift from personal- to system-based trust also has implications for trust breach and repair. In the case of a breach, it is usually more difficult to clearly locate responsibilities under system trust than under interpersonal trust. The cause of the breach is often causally ambiguous within the system. Moreover, the impact of a system trust breach could be far more severe than that of an interpersonal trust breach. For these reasons, our practical and conceptual understanding of trust breach and repair is not readily transferrable from the interpersonal to the system level (Gillespie & Dietz, 2009). It is thus important to understand what mechanisms should be put in place to prevent a system-level trust breach of blockchains. We also need to understand the most effective trust repair practices in the event of a system-level failure, such as The DAO hack. Traditional trust repair processes (e.g., developing shared mental models and deepening the relationship) cannot be easily implemented with distant trustees. A new line of research into the repair of system trust thus seems warranted.

Scholars have widely acknowledged that trustworthiness could be an important source of competitive advantage (Barney & Hansen, 1994; Schilke & Cook, 2015). Therefore, organizations need to understand how to improve their perceived trustworthiness among stakeholders. Zucker (1986) identifies three modes of trust production for personal trust: process-based (i.e., trust can be developed based on past or expected exchanges between collaborating parties), characteristic-based (i.e., trust can be developed based on a party's personal characteristics such as belonging to a certain social category), and institution-based (trust can be developed based on societal institution arrangements). However, since the major form of trust shifts from personal trust to system trust in the context of blockchains, these three modes of trust production may be less relevant. Organizations need to rethink their strategies in building trustworthiness. Scholars should revise and extend Zucker's framework of trust production modes of personal trust to system trust to deepen the understanding of the approaches in which trust in systems is produced.

Finally, blockchains can shift the target of trust. This shift requires people to trust others whom they have not met before. Developing initial trust is critical here – we need to understand how people develop judgements of the trustworthiness of those they are not familiar with, including the developers of the codes and the entities that provide information feeds to blockchains. Signalling theory may be particularly relevant to help scholars understand the kinds of signals that would be interpreted by the users of blockchains as credible enough and that less trustworthy trustees could not easily send (Gambetta, 2009; Spence, 1973).

### 6.2.3 An Agenda for Blockchains and Organizational Design Research

The various implications of blockchains for organizational design bring up interesting research opportunities. Despite some scholarly research (e.g., DuPont, 2017; Hsieh et al., 2018; Murray et al., 2021a), our understanding of DAOs still needs to be deepened. As a new form of organization that works differently from traditional forms, we need to understand how the unique ways of organizing activities in a DAO impact collaborative dynamics and performance. A recent study by Zhao and colleagues (2022) provides a useful investigation on this issue. Tracking the voting activities of participants of MakerDAO, they show that the performance of the DAO will benefit more from distributing strategic decisions (i.e., decisions that focus on longer-term impact, such as system upgrades and personnel change) rather than operational decisions (i.e., decisions that focus on short-term efficiency, such as adjusting parameters in the business processes). Such effects will be moderated by other design features of the DAO organization, including task allocation, reward distribution, and information provision.

On the flip side, to better grasp the uniqueness of blockchain-based decentralized organizations, we need to understand how DAOs differ from other forms of so-called decentralized organizations, such as traditional flat structures and empowerment of decision-making rights within an organization, and, more recently, open-source project development. The study by Vergne (2020) provides a useful starting point by clarifying the very meaning of the term 'decentralization'. Distinguishing decentralization from distribution, he suggests that many platform companies, such as Uber and Facebook, are indeed highly centralized, contrary to what they claim to be.

Understanding such differences will help scholars elucidate the boundary conditions of proper choices of different organizational forms. Traditional hierarchical organizational forms will surely not become obsolete in the near future. However, it would be useful to better understand the conditions under which DAOs can be a viable organizational form. Specifically, scholars should ask what makes DAOs superior to traditional organizational choices – and vice versa. For example, although decentralized decision-making is attractive in many aspects, centralized organizing can be more efficient because it can make good use of superior knowledge, experience, and vision residing in higher hierarchical positions. Such comparative analyses should be helpful in answering questions about the kinds of tasks that are most suitable to be organized via DAOs, thereby furthering our understanding of the trade-offs of various organizational forms under different circumstances.

Scholars could also investigate the evolution of the role of managers in blockchain-supported organizations. Different types of managers might be impacted differently. For example, since blockchains can help facilitate the reliable execution of operations, middle managers whose major tasks are verifying and monitoring may become less important. Top managers will be freed from excessive monitoring tasks as well, which will give them time to refocus on high-level issues, such as organizational design and strategy.

The diffusion of blockchains within organizations also creates a demand for different skill sets, if not new jobs. The combination of a good understanding of business processes and blockchain-related technical skills will become particularly important. Managers with expertise at the interface of the technical and legal features of blockchains are likely to be highly sought after. In turn, this evolution will call for universities and training institutes to update their curriculum to cover these new interfaces.

## 6.3 The Future of Blockchains

Blockchain technology still has a long way to maturity. The business world has continued to explore different blockchain possibilities and best practices. Despite the fact that firms currently lean more towards adopting permissioned blockchains, many practitioners and academics believe that permissionless blockchains are the way of the future. The major reason is that building private blockchain networks is expensive and complicated and makes attracting a large number of users challenging. Similarly, the difficulty of realizing interoperability also limits the prospects of permissioned blockchains (EY, 2020). Indeed, the issue of interoperability across different blockchain systems may be 'the most important one to solve to truly realize an "Internet of values"' (Lacity, 2020, p. 311). To fully realize the prospects of the Fourth Industrial Revolution (Jazdi, 2014; Schwab, 2017), blockchains should not be viewed as stand-alone solutions but be effectively integrated with other technologies, such as EDI, AI, and the Internet of Things (IoT).

The combination of EDI and blockchains affords the ability to ensure higher security and generate fewer errors along the supply chain (Fiaidhi et al., 2018). EDI standardizes digital information from different sources, allowing organizations to exchange information between their customized enterprise resource planning (ERP) systems. EDI standards will continue to be useful to reduce costs along the supply chain, and blockchains may add to that a new transmission medium of EDI files (Mani, 2019). This new transmission medium can produce a single version of the truth for the EDI files being transmitted, thereby reducing inconsistencies and increasing security. It can also process the data with smart contracts. One example is the IBM Food Trust blockchain, which uses EDI standards to shape the data and record them via blockchain protocols.

Blockchains are thus complementary to EDI, and the combination of these technologies can potentially result in much more efficient, transparent, and secure global supply chains (Centobelli et al., 2021).

The integration of blockchains and AI can also provide promising benefits. AI technologies (e.g., machine learning) use accessible data to improve existing algorithms and make decisions automatically. The quality of inputs largely determines the effectiveness of training AI models and, thus, the validity of the outputs of AI applications. Blockchains can be complementary to AI, as they enable transparent and trustworthy information recording to feed reliable data to AI algorithms (Angelis & da Silva, 2019). In addition, blockchains can record the outputs of AI applications in a decentralized network, which protects both the security and privacy of clients (Salah et al., 2019). Conversely, AI can be useful for blockchains in further automating decision-making processes by contributing intelligence and analytics. For example, in the procurement block-chain deployed by the United States. GSA, AI is combined with a blockchain to automate processes in governmental procurement, such as vendor assessment (Nayak & Nguyen, 2018).

IoT technologies and blockchains are also useful complements to one another. On the one hand, IoT devices can (semi)automatically collect information and exchange data with each other. Reliable and widely spread IoT devices may substantially reduce potential mistakes by human agents, either conscious or inadvertent. This reduction may, in turn, greatly enhance the quality of the information feed for blockchains and lessen 'garbage in, garbage out' concerns (Halaburda, 2018). On the other hand, blockchains can be an ideal mechanism for data storage and reporting for IoT systems. By creating tamper-resistant records of data, blockchains can maintain the integrity of a network of IoT devices, preventing malicious nodes from contaminating the IoT environment (Fortino et al., 2020). With the advent of the Fourth Industrial Revolution, the successful integration of blockchains and IoT technologies will be the funda-mental infrastructure for realizing the goal of automation across organizations (Schwab, 2017). We are excited to see how such combinations facilitate the implementation of important worldwide initiatives (e.g., the United Nations' Sustainable Development Goals, De Villiers et al., 2021) that may elevate living standards on a global scale.

## 6.4 Summary

Blockchains are among the most disruptive new technologies of recent times, with potentially significant impacts on the future of the economy and society. Managers need to stay abreast of the latest developments in blockchains to ensure that their firms remain competitive, and management scholars can provide important insights by elucidating the organizational implications that blockchains will bring about. We hope that this Element provides a useful starting point for both audiences in embracing this exciting new phenomenon. We envision this Element as a thought-provoking examination of contemporary discussions about blockchains along with their opportunities and challenges and as a springboard for future examinations. We look forward to witnessing the evolution of blockchains in the years to come.

# References

Adhami, S., Giudici, G., & Martinazzi, S. (2018). Why do businesses go crypto? An empirical analysis of initial coin offerings. *Journal of Economics and Business*, 100, 64–75.

Ahluwalia, S., Mahto, R. V., & Guerrero, M. (2020). Blockchain technology and startup financing: A transaction cost economics perspective. *Technological Forecasting and Social Change*, 151, 119854.

Akyildirim, E., Corbet, S., Cumming, D., Lucey, B., & Sensoy, A. (2020). Riding the wave of crypto-exuberance: The potential misusage of corporate blockchain announcements. *Technological Forecasting and Social Change*, 159, 120191.

Alabi, K. (2017). Digital blockchain networks appear to be following Metcalfe's Law. *Electronic Commerce Research and Applications*, 24, 23–9.

Alexandre, A. (2018). New study says 80 percent of ICOs conducted in 2017 were scams. *Cointelegraph*. Accessed 17 June 2021. https://cointelegraph.com/news/new-study-says-80-percent-of-icos-conducted-in-2017-were-scams.

Allen, D. W., Berg, C., Markey-Towler, B., Novak, M., & Potts, J. (2020). Blockchain and the evolution of institutional technologies: Implications for innovation policy. *Research Policy*, 49(1), 103865.

Angelis, J., & da Silva, E. R. (2019). Blockchain adoption: A value driver perspective. *Business Horizons*, 62(3), 307–14.

Antonopoulos, A. M. (2014). *Mastering Bitcoin: Unlocking Digital Cryptocurrencies*. Sebastopol, CA: O'Reilly Media.

Aratani, L. (2021). Electricity needed to mine Bitcoin is more than used by entire countries. *The Guardian*. Accessed 2 June 2021. www.theguardian.com/technology/2021/feb/27/bitcoin-mining-electricity-use-environmental-impact.

Arrowsmith, R. (2021). EY and Microsoft expand Xbox blockchain smart contract platform. *Accounting Today*. Accessed 22 May 2021. www.accountingtoday.com/news/ey-and-microsoft-expand-xbox-blockchain-smart-contract-platform.

Babich, V., & Hilary, G. (2020). OM Forum – Distributed ledgers and operations: What operations management researchers should know about blockchain technology. *Manufacturing & Service Operations Management*, 22(2), 223–40.

Bahga, A., & Madisetti, V. K. (2016). Blockchain platform for industrial Internet of Things. *Journal of Software Engineering and Applications*, 9 (10), 533–46.

Bai, C., & Sarkis, J. (2020). A supply chain transparency and sustainability technology appraisal model for blockchain technology. *International Journal of Production Research*, 58(7), 2142–62.

Bambrough, B. (2020). Massive hack exposes Bitcoin's greatest weakness. *Forbes*. Accessed 21 June 2021. www.forbes.com/sites/billybambrough/2020/12/23/massive-hack-exposes-bitcoins-greatest-weakness/?sh=2f28b579da7d.

Barney, J. (1991). Firm resources and sustained competitive advantage. *Journal of Management*, 17(1), 99–120.

Barney, J. B., & Hansen, M. H. (1994). Trustworthiness as a source of competitive advantage. *Strategic Management Journal*, 15(8), 175–90.

Beck, R., Müller-Bloch, C., & King, J. L. (2018). Governance in the blockchain economy: A framework and research agenda. *Journal of the Association for Information Systems*, 19(10), 1020–34.

Bergin, T., & Layne, N. (2015). Special report: Cyber thieves exploit banks' faith in SWIFT transfer network. *Reuters*. Accessed 2 June 2021. www.reuters.com/article/us-cyber-heist-swift-specialreport-idUSKCN0YB0DD.

Bertino, E., Kundu, A., & Sura, Z. (2019). Data transparency with blockchain and AI ethics. *Journal of Data and Information Quality*, 11(4), 1–8.

Bodkhe, U., Mehta, D., Tanwar, S. et al. (2020). A survey on decentralized consensus mechanisms for cyber physical systems. *IEEE Access*, 8, 54371–401.

Bouri, E., Shahzad, S. J. H., & Roubaud, D. (2019). Co-explosivity in the cryptocurrency market. *Finance Research Letters*, 29, 178–83.

Brink, S. (2021). How can blockchain support the energy transition? *Shell*. Accessed 21 June 2021. www.shell.com/energy-and-innovation/digitalisation/news-room/blockchain-building-trust-to-enable-the-energy-transition.html.

Burns, J., Steele, A., Cohen, E. E., & Ramamoorti, S. (2020). Blockchain and internal control: A COSO perspective. *COSO*. Accessed 21 June 2021. www.aicpa.org/content/dam/aicpa/interestareas/informationtechnology/downloadabledocuments/blockchain-and-internal-control-the-coso-perspective.pdf.

Buterin, V. (2014). A next-generation smart contract and decentralized application platform. *Ethereum Whitepaper*. Accessed 21 June 2021. https://blockchainlab.com/pdf/Ethereum_white_paper-a_next_generation_smart_contract_and_decentralized_application_platform-vitalik-buterin.pdf.

Cai, Y. J., Choi, T. M., & Zhang, J. (2021). Platform supported supply chain operations in the blockchain era: Supply contracting and moral hazards. *Decision Sciences*, 52(4), 866–92.

Cao, Z., Li, Y., Jayaram, J., Liu, Y., & Lumineau, F. (2018). A meta-analysis of the exchange hazards–interfirm governance relationship: An informal institutions perspective. *Journal of International Business Studies*, 49(3), 303–23.

Cao, Z., & Lumineau, F. (2015). Revisiting the interplay between contractual and relational governance: A qualitative and meta-analytic investigation. *Journal of Operations Management*, 33–34, 15–42.

Carson, B., Romanelli, G., Walsh, P., & Zhumaev, A. (2018). Blockchain beyond the hype: What is the strategic business value? *McKinsey & Company*. Accessed 22 April 2022. www.caba.org/wp-content/uploads/2020/04/IS-2018-209.pdf.

Casey, M. J., & Vigna, P. (2018). In blockchain we trust. *MIT Technology Review*, 121(3), 10–16.

Catalini, C., & Gans, J. S. (2016). Some simple economics of the blockchain. *National Bureau of Economic Research*. Accessed 21 June 2021. www.nber.org/papers/w22952.

CBInsights. (2019). How blockchain could disrupt insurance. Accessed 21 June 2021. www.cbinsights.com/research/blockchain-insurance-disruption/.

Cennamo, C., Marchesi, C., & Meyer, T. (2020). Two sides of the same coin? Decentralized versus proprietary blockchains and the performance of digital currencies. *Academy of Management Discoveries*, 6(3), 382–405.

Centobelli, P., Cerchione, R., Del Vecchio, P., Oropallo, E., & Secundo, G. (2021). Blockchain technology for bridging trust, traceability and transparency in circular supply chain. *Information & Management*, forthcoming. https://doi.org/10.1016/j.im.2021.103508.

Chalmers, D., Matthews, R., & Hyslop, A. (2021). Blockchain as an external enabler of new venture ideas: Digital entrepreneurs and the disintermediation of the global music industry. *Journal of Business Research*, 125(5), 577–91.

Chang, V., Baudier, P., Zhang, H. et al. (2020a). How blockchain can impact financial services: The overview, challenges and recommendations from expert interviewees. *Technological Forecasting and Social Change*, 158, 120166.

Chang, Y., Iakovou, E., & Shi, W. (2020b). Blockchain in global supply chains and cross border trade: A critical synthesis of the state-of-the-art, challenges and opportunities. *International Journal of Production Research*, 58(7), 2082–99.

Chen, H., Pendleton, M., Njilla, L., & Xu, S. (2020). A survey on Ethereum systems security: Vulnerabilities, attacks, and defenses. *ACM Computing Surveys*, 53(3), Article 67. https://doi.org/10.1145/3391195.

Chen, Y. (2018). Blockchain tokens and the potential democratization of entrepreneurship and innovation. *Business Horizons*, 61(4), 567–75.

Chen, Y., Pereira, I., & Patel, P. C. (2021). Decentralized governance of digital platforms. *Journal of Management*, 47(5), 1305–37.

Cheng, S. F., De Franco, G., Jiang, H., & Lin, P. (2019). Riding the blockchain mania: Public firms' speculative 8-K disclosures. *Management Science*, 65 (12), 5901–13.

Chod, J., Trichakis, N., Tsoukalas, G., Aspegren, H., & Weber, M. (2020). On the financing benefits of supply chain transparency and blockchain adoption. *Management Science*, 66(10), 4378–96.

Clemons, E. K., Reddi, S. P., & Row, M. C. (1993). The impact of information technology on the organization of economic activity: The 'move to the middle' hypothesis. *Journal of Management Information Systems*, 10(2), 9–35.

Clohessy, T., & Acton, T. (2019). Investigating the influence of organizational factors on blockchain adoption: An innovation theory perspective. *Industrial Management & Data Systems*, 119(7), 1457–91.

Cole, R., Stevenson, M., & Aitken, J. (2019). Blockchain technology: Implications for operations and supply chain management. *Supply Chain Management: An International Journal*, 24(4), 469–83.

Cong, L. W., & He, Z. (2019). Blockchain disruption and smart contracts. *Review of Financial Studies*, 32(5), 1754–97.

Criddle, C. (2021). Bitcoin consumes 'more electricity than Argentina'. *BBC News*. Accessed 2 June 2021. www.bbc.com/news/technology-56012952.

Damsgaard, J., & Lyytinen, K. (1998). Contours of diffusion of electronic data interchange in Finland: Overcoming technological barriers and collaborating to make it happen. *Journal of Strategic Information Systems*, 7(4), 275–97.

Das, T. K., & Teng, B. S. (1998). Between trust and control: Developing confidence in partner cooperation in alliances. *Academy of Management Review*, 23(3), 491–512.

Davidson, S., De Filippi, P., & Potts, J. (2018). Blockchains and the economic institutions of capitalism. *Journal of Institutional Economics*, 14(4), 639–58.

De Filippi, P., Mannan, M., & Reijers, W. (2020). Blockchain as a confidence machine: The problem of trust & challenges of governance. *Technology in Society*, 62, 101284.

De Filippi, P., & Wright, A. (2018). *Blockchain and the Law: The Rule of Code*. Cambridge, MA: Harvard University Press.

De Villiers, C., Kuruppu, S., & Dissanayake, D. (2021). A (new) role for business: Promoting the United Nations' Sustainable Development Goals through the internet-of-things and blockchain technology. *Journal of Business Research*, 131, 598–609.

Deloitte. (2020). Deloitte's 2020 global blockchain survey. Accessed 2 June 2021. www2.deloitte.com/content/dam/insights/us/articles/

6608_2020-global-blockchain-survey/DI_CIR%202020%20global% 20blockchain%20survey.pdf.

Dierksmeier, C., & Seele, P. (2018). Cryptocurrencies and business ethics. *Journal of Business Ethics*, 152(1), 1–14.

Dierksmeier, C., & Seele, P. (2020). Blockchain and business ethics. *Business Ethics: A European Review*, 29(2), 348–59.

Du, W. D., Pan, S. L., Leidner, D. E., & Ying, W. (2019). Affordances, experimentation and actualization of FinTech: A blockchain implementation study. *Journal of Strategic Information Systems*, 28(1), 50–65.

Duncan, S. (2019). Privacy on public blockchains: EY clients and the blockchain curious must leverage this 'best of both worlds' breakthrough. *EY*. Accessed 30 April 2021. https://assets.ey.com/content/dam/ey-sites/ey-com/ en_gl/generic/ey-2019-hfs-report-privacy-on-public-blockchains.pdf.

DuPont, Q. (2017). Experiments in algorithmic governance: A history and ethnography of 'The DAO', a failed decentralized autonomous organization, in Campbell-Verduyn, M. (ed.), *Bitcoin and Beyond*. New York: Routledge, 157–77.

Durovic, M., & Janssen, A. (2019). Formation of smart contracts under contract law. in DiMatteo, L., Cannarsa, M., & Poncibo, C. (eds.), *The Cambridge Handbook of Smart Contracts, Blockchain Technology and Digital Platforms (Cambridge Law Handbooks)*. Cambridge: Cambridge University Press, 61–79.

Emmelhainz, M. A. (1988). Strategic issues of EDI implementation. *Journal of Business Logistics*, 9(2), 55–70.

Ennis, M. (2021). NFT art: The bizarre world where burning a Banksy can make it more valuable. *The Conversation*. Accessed 18 June 2021. https:// theconversation.com/nft-art-the-bizarre-world-where-burning-a-banksy-can-make-it-more-valuable-156605#:~:text=A%20blockchain%20company%20has %20bought,from%20a%20New%20York%20gallery.

Ethereum. (2021). Proof-of-stake (POS). Accessed 17 June 2021. https://ether eum.org/en/developers/docs/consensus-mechanisms/pos/.

EY. (2020). Seize the day: Public blockchain is on the horizon. Accessed 2 June 2021. https://assets.ey.com/content/dam/ey-sites/ey-com/en_gl/ topics/blockchain/ey-public-blockchain-opportunity-snapshot.pdf.

Fanning, K., & Centers, D. P. (2016). Blockchain and its coming impact on financial services. *Journal of Corporate Accounting & Finance*, 27(5), 53–7.

Felin, T., & Lakhani, K. (2018). What problems will you solve with blockchain? *MIT Sloan Management Review*, 60(1), 32–8.

Fernandez-Carames, T. M., & Fraga-Lamas, P. (2020). Towards post-quantum blockchain: A review on blockchain cryptography resistant to quantum computing attacks. *IEEE Access*, 8, 21091–116.

Fiaidhi, J., Mohammed, S., & Mohammed, S. (2018). EDI with blockchain as an enabler for extreme automation. *IT Professional*, 20(4), 66–72.

Fisch, C., & Momtaz, P. P. (2020). Institutional investors and post-ICO performance: An empirical analysis of investor returns in initial coin offerings (ICOs). *Journal of Corporate Finance*, 64, 101679.

Forde, E. (2021). Cash 'gifts' and strong-arm tactics: Music's problem with NFTs. *The Guardian*. Accessed 30 July 2022.www.theguardian.com/music/2021/apr/07/cash-gifts-and-strong-arm-tactics-musics-problem-with-nfts.

Fortino, G., Messina, F., Rosaci, D., & Sarné, G. M. (2020). Using blockchain in a reputation-based model for grouping agents in the Internet of Things. *IEEE Transactions on Engineering Management*, 67(4), 1231–43.

Fry, J., & Cheah, E. T. (2016). Negative bubbles and shocks in cryptocurrency markets. *International Review of Financial Analysis*, 47, 343–52.

Fulmer, C. A., & Gelfand, M. J. (2012). At what level (and in whom) we trust: Trust across multiple organizational levels. *Journal of Management*, 38(4), 1167–230.

Gambetta, D. (2009). Signaling, in Hedström, P., & Bearman, P. (eds.), *The Oxford Handbook of Analytical Sociology*. New York: Oxford University Press, 168–94.

Garay, J., Kiayias, A., & Leonardos, N. (2015). The Bitcoin backbone protocol: Analysis and applications, in Oswald, E., & Fischlin, M. (eds.), *Advances in Cryptology – EUROCRYPT 2015*. Berlin: Springer, 281–310.

Garg, P., Gupta, B., Chauhan, A. K. et al. (2021). Measuring the perceived benefits of implementing blockchain technology in the banking sector. *Technological Forecasting and Social Change*, 163, 120407.

Gaszcz, C. (2019). Hyundai division is developing a blockchain platform to track history of used cars. *Yahoo*. Accessed 23 April 2022. www.yahoo.com/video/hyundai-division-developing-blockchain-platform-105745154.html.

Gillespie, N., & Dietz, G. (2009). Trust repair after an organization-level failure. *Academy of Management Review*, 34(1), 127–45.

Giudici, G., & Adhami, S. (2019). The impact of governance signals on ICO fundraising success. *Journal of Industrial and Business Economics*, 46(2), 283–312.

Gleim, M. R., & Stevens, J. L. (2021). Blockchain: A game changer for marketers? *Marketing Letters*, 32(1), 123–8.

Glikson, E., & Woolley, A. W. (2020). Human trust in artificial intelligence: Review of empirical research. *Academy of Management Annals*, 14(2), 627–60.

Goldsby, C., & Hanisch, M. (2022). The boon and bane of blockchain: Getting the governance right. *California Management Review*, 64(3), 141–68.

Gulati, R., Wohlgezogen, F., & Zhelyazkov, P. (2012). The two facets of collaboration: Cooperation and coordination in strategic alliances. *Academy of Management Annals*, 6(1), 531–83.

Halaburda, H. (2018). Blockchain revolution without the blockchain? *Communications of the ACM*, 61(7), 27–9.

Halaburda, H., Haeringer, G., Gans, J. S., & Gandal, N. (2020). The microeconomics of cryptocurrencies. *National Bureau of Economic Research*. Accessed 30 July 2022. www.nber.org/system/files/working_papers/w27477/w27477.pdf.

Halaburda, H., & Mueller-Bloch, C. (2020). Toward a multidimensional conceptualization of decentralization in blockchain governance: Commentary on 'two sides of the same coin? Decentralized versus proprietary blockchains and the performance of digital currencies' by Cennamo, Marchesi, & Meyer. *Academy of Management Discoveries*, 6(4), 712–14.

Hanisch, M., Theodosiadis, V., & Teixeira, F. (2022). Digital governance: How blockchain technologies revolutionize the governance of interorganizational relationships, in Baalmans, S., Broekhuizen, T., & Fabian, N. (eds.), *Digital Transformation*. Groningen: University of Groningen Press, forthcoming. https://research.rug.nl/en/publications/digital-governance-how-blockchain-technologies-revolutionize-the-.

Hasan, M. R., Shiming, D., Islam, M. A., & Hossain, M. Z. (2020). Operational efficiency effects of blockchain technology implementation in firms. *Review of International Business and Strategy*, 30(2), 163–81.

Hertig, A. (2020). What is an oracle? *CoinDesk*. Accessed 22 May 2021. www .coindesk.com/what-is-an-oracle.

Hojckova, K., Ahlborg, H., Morrison, G. M., & Sandén, B. (2020). Entrepreneurial use of context for technological system creation and expansion: The case of blockchain-based peer-to-peer electricity trading. *Research Policy*, 49(8), 104046.

Hooper, A., & Holtbrügge, D. (2020). Blockchain technology in international business: Changing the agenda for global governance. *Review of International Business and Strategy*, 30(2), 183–200.

Hsieh, Y. Y., Vergne, J. P., Anderson, P., Lakhani, K., & Reitzig, M. (2018). Bitcoin and the rise of decentralized autonomous organizations. *Journal of Organization Design*, 7, 14. https://doi.org/10.1186/s41469-018-0038-1.

Hsieh, Y. Y., Vergne, J. P., & Wang, S. (2017). The internal and external governance of blockchain-based organizations, in Campbell-Verduyn, M. (ed.), *Bitcoin and Beyond*. New York: Routledge, 48–68.

Huang, L., Röck, D., Murray, A., & Hofmann, E. (2020). *modum.io: Funding a Blockchain-Based Start-Up's Supply Chain Solution*. Boston, MA: Harvard Business School.

Huang, R. (2019). UN pilot in Mongolia uses blockchain to help farmers deliver sustainable cashmere. *Forbes*. Accessed 11 May 2021. www.forbes.com/sites/rogerhuang/2019/12/28/un-pilot-in-mongolia-uses-blockchain-to-help-farmers-deliver-sustainable-cashmere/?sh=70e0262517d9.

IBM. (2020). Blockchain and the unbanked: Changes coming to global finance. Accessed 18 June 2021. www.ibm.com/blogs/blockchain/2020/03/block chain-and-the-unbanked-changes-coming-to-global-finance/.

IBM. (2021). Building trust and transparency in insurance policies with block-chain. Accessed 22 May 2021. https://mediacenter.ibm.com/id/1_ovxiynn1.

Iftody, E. (2019). What's the difference between Crowdfunding, ICO's, IEO's and STO's? *Medium*. Accessed 21 June 2021. https://medium.com/swlh/whats-the-difference-between-crowdfunding-ico-s-ieo-s-and-sto-s-d4059f6b24ed.

Jain, A., & Jain, C. (2019). Blockchain hysteria: Adding 'blockchain' to company's name. *Economics Letters*, 181, 178–81.

Jaoude, J., & Saade, R. G. (2019). Blockchain applications – Usage in different domains. *IEEE Access*, 7, 45360–81.

Jazdi, N. (2014). Cyber physical systems in the context of Industry 4.0, in Miclea, L., & Stoian, I. (eds.), *2014 IEEE International Conference on Automation, Quality and Testing, Robotics*. Cluj-Napoca: IEEE, 1–4. https://doi.org/10.1109/AQTR.2014.6857843.

Jensen, M. C., & Meckling, W. H. (1976). Theory of the firm: Managerial behavior, agency costs and ownership structure. *Journal of Financial Economics*, 3(4), 305–60.

Kamble, S., Gunasekaran, A., & Arha, H. (2019). Understanding the blockchain technology adoption in supply chains-Indian context. *International Journal of Production Research*, 57(7), 2009–33.

Khanna, T., Gulati, R., & Nohria, N. (1998). The dynamics of learning alliances: Competition, cooperation, and relative scope. *Strategic Management Journal*, 19(3), 193–210.

Kiktenko, E. O., Pozhar, N. O., Anufriev, M. N. et al. (2018). Quantum-secured blockchain. *Quantum Science and Technology*, 3(3), 035004.

Kim, S. K., & Huh, J. H. (2020). Blockchain of carbon trading for UN sustainable development goals. *Sustainability*, 12(10), 4021.

Knill, E. (2010). Quantum computing. *Nature*, 463, 441–3.

Koufaris, M., & Hampton-Sosa, W. (2004). The development of initial trust in an online company by new customers. *Information & Management*, 41(3), 377–97.

Kurpjuweit, S., Schmidt, C. G., Klöckner, M., & Wagner, S. M. (2021). Blockchain in additive manufacturing and its impact on supply chains. *Journal of Business Logistics*, 42(1), 46–70.

Lacity, M., & van Hoek, R. (2021a). Requiem for reconciliations: DL Freight, a blockchain-enabled solution by Walmart Canada and DLT Labs. *Blockchain Center of Excellence*. Accessed 2 June 2021. https://blockchain.uark.edu/new-bcoe-white-paper-on-walmart-canada-dlt-labs/.

Lacity, M., & van Hoek, R. (2021b). What we've learned so far about blockchain for business. *MIT Sloan Management Review*, 62(3), 48–54.

Lacity, M. C. (2020). *Blockchain Foundations: For the Internet of Value*. Arkansas: Epic Books.

Lee, I., & Shin, Y. J. (2018). Fintech: Ecosystem, business models, investment decisions, and challenges. *Business Horizons*, 61(1), 35–46.

Leising, M. (2017). The $55M hack that almost brought Ethereum down. *CoinDesk*. Accessed 17 June 2021. www.coindesk.com/tech/2020/09/17/the-55m-hack-that-almost-brought-ethereum-down/.

Leonard, J. (2019). For blockchain it's time to face up to governance and regulation. *Computing*. Accessed 18 June 2021. www.computing.co.uk/analysis/3076512/for-blockchain-its-time-to-face-up-to-governance-and-regulation.

Lewis, J. D., & Weigert, A. (1985). Trust as a social reality. *Social Forces*, 63 (4), 967–85.

Li, J. J., Poppo, L., & Zhou, K. Z. (2010). Relational mechanisms, formal contracts, and local knowledge acquisition by international subsidiaries. *Strategic Management Journal*, 31(4), 349–70.

Liang, T. P., Kohli, R., Huang, H. C., & Li, Z. L. (2021). What drives the adoption of the blockchain technology? A fit-viability perspective. *Journal of Management Information Systems*, 38(2), 314–37.

Liu, Y., & Tsyvinski, A. (2021). Risks and returns of cryptocurrency. *Review of Financial Studies*, 34(6), 2689–727.

Liu, Z., & Li, Z. (2020). A blockchain-based framework of cross-border e-commerce supply chain. *International Journal of Information Management*, 52, 102059.

Long, C. P., & Sitkin, S. B. (2018). Control–trust dynamics in organizations: Identifying shared perspectives and charting conceptual fault lines. *Academy of Management Annals*, 12(2), 725–51.

Long, C. P., & Weibel, A. (2018). Two sides of an important coin: Outlining the general parameters of control-trust research, in Searle, R., Nienaber, A. M., & Sitkin, S. B. (eds.), *The Routledge Companion to Trust*. New York: Routledge, 506–21.

Luhmann, N. (1979). *Trust and Power*. Chichester: Wiley.

Lumineau, F., & Malhotra, D. (2011). Shadow of the contract: How contract structure shapes inter-firm dispute resolution. *Strategic Management Journal*, 32(5), 532–55.

Lumineau, F., Wang, W., & Schilke, O. (2021a). Blockchain governance – A new way of organizing collaborations? *Organization Science*, 32(2), 500–21.

Lumineau, F., Wang, W., & Schilke, O. (2021b). Blockchains can change the way we collaborate. *LSE Business Review*. Accessed 30 July 2022. https://blogs.lse.ac.uk/businessreview/2021/01/14/blockchains-can-change-the-way-we-collaborate/.

Lumineau, F., Wang, W., Schilke, O., & Huang, L. (2021c). How blockchain can simplify partnerships. *Harvard Business Review*. Accessed 30 July 2022. https://hbr.org/2021/04/how-blockchain-can-simplify-partnerships.

Macneil, I. R. (1978). Contracts: Adjustment of long-term economic relations under classical, neoclassical, and relational contract law. *Northwestern University Law Review*, 72, 854–902.

Makarov, I., & Schoar, A. (2020). Trading and arbitrage in cryptocurrency markets. *Journal of Financial Economics*, 135(2), 293–319.

Malhotra, A., O'Neill, H., & Stowell, P. (2022). Thinking strategically about blockchain adoption and risk mitigation. *Business Horizons*, 65(2), 159–71.

Malhotra, D., & Lumineau, F. (2011). Trust and collaboration in the aftermath of conflict: The effects of contract structure. *Academy of Management Journal*, 54(5), 981–98.

Mani, K. (2019). Will blockchain replace EDI? Yes and no. *Forbes*. Accessed 22 April 2022. www.forbes.com/sites/forbestechcouncil/2019/04/03/will-blockchain-replace-edi-yes-and-no/?sh=55ef370347d7.

Mattke, J., Hund, A., Maier, C., & Weitzel, T. (2019). How an enterprise blockchain application in the US pharmaceuticals supply chain is saving lives. *MIS Quarterly Executive*, 18(4), 245–61.

Matzutt, R., Hiller, J., Henze, M. et al. (2018). A quantitative analysis of the impact of arbitrary blockchain content on Bitcoin, in Meiklejohn, S., & Sako, K. (eds.), *Financial Cryptography and Data Security*. Berlin: Springer, 420–38.

Mayer, K. J., & Argyres, N. S. (2004). Learning to contract: Evidence from the personal computer industry. *Organization Science*, 15(4), 394–410.

Mayer, R. C., Davis, J. H., & Schoorman, F. D. (1995). An integrative model of organizational trust. *Academy of Management Review*, 20(3), 709–34.

McKnight, D. H., Carter, M., Thatcher, J. B., & Clay, P. F. (2011). Trust in a specific technology: An investigation of its components and measures. *ACM Transactions on Management Information Systems*, 2(2), 1–25.

Mohan, V. (2019). On the use of blockchain-based mechanisms to tackle academic misconduct. *Research Policy*, 48(9), 103805.

Montecchi, M., Plangger, K., & Etter, M. (2019). It's real, trust me! Establishing supply chain provenance using blockchain. *Business Horizons*, 62(3), 283–93.

Murray, A., Kuban, S., Josefy, M., & Anderson, J. (2021a). Contracting in the smart era: The implications of blockchain and decentralized autonomous organizations for contracting and corporate governance. *Academy of Management Perspectives*, 35(4), 622–41.

Murray, A., Rhymer, J., & Sirmon, D. G. (2021b). Humans and technology: Forms of conjoined agency in organizations. *Academy of Management Review*, 46(3), 552–71.

Nakamoto, S. (2008). Bitcoin: A peer-to-peer electronic cash system. *Bitcoin. org.* Accessed 18 June 2021. https://bitcoin.org/bitcoin.pdf.

Nandi, M. L., Nandi, S., Moya, H., & Kaynak, H. (2020). Blockchain technology-enabled supply chain systems and supply chain performance: A resource-based view. *Supply Chain Management: An International Journal*, 25(6), 841–62.

Nandi, S., Sarkis, J., Hervani, A., & Helms, M. (2021). Do blockchain and circular economy practices improve post COVID-19 supply chains? A resource-based and resource dependence perspective. *Industrial Management & Data Systems*, 121(2), 333–63.

Narayanan, A., & Clark, J. (2017). Bitcoin's academic pedigree. *Communications of the ACM*, 60(12), 36–45.

Nayak, N., & Nguyen, D. T. (2018). Blockchain, AI and robotics: How future tech will simplify federal procurement. *Federal Times*. Accessed 21 June 2021. www.federaltimes.com/acquisition/2018/03/23/blockchain-ai-and-robotics-how-future-tech-will-simplify-federal-procurement/.

New York Times. (2021). Dealbook newsletter: When doing well means doing good. Accessed 21 June 2021. www.nytimes.com/2021/03/15/business/deal book/sec-esg-priority.html.

Niranjanamurthy, M., Nithya, B. N., & Jagannatha, S. (2019). Analysis of blockchain technology: Pros, cons and SWOT. *Cluster Computing*, 22(6), 14743–57.

Okhuysen, G. A., & Bechky, B. A. (2009). Coordination in organizations: An integrative perspective. *Academy of Management Annals*, 3(1), 463–502.

Oprunenco, A., & Akmeemana, C. (2018). Using blockchain to make land registry more reliable in India. *LSE Business Review*. Accessed 30 July 2022. https://blogs.lse.ac.uk/businessreview/2018/04/13/using-block chain-to-make-land-registry-more-reliable-in-india/.

Oxley, J. E. (1999). Institutional environment and the mechanisms of governance: The impact of intellectual property protection on the structure of inter-firm alliances. *Journal of Economic Behavior & Organization*, 38(3), 283–309.

Palmer, D. (2016). 7 cool decentralized apps being built on Ethereum. *CoinDesk*. Accessed 21 June 2021. www.coindesk.com/7-cool-decentralized-apps-built-ethereum.

Park, G., Shin, S. R., & Choy, M. (2020). Early mover (dis) advantages and knowledge spillover effects on blockchain startups' funding and innovation performance. *Journal of Business Research*, 109, 64–75.

Parkhe, A. (1993). Strategic alliance structuring: A game theoretic and transaction cost examination of interfirm cooperation. *Academy of Management Journal*, 36(4), 794–829.

Parmigiani, A., & Rivera-Santos, M. (2015). Sourcing for the base of the pyramid: Constructing supply chains to address voids in subsistence markets. *Journal of Operations Management*, 33–34, 60–70.

Pazaitis, A., De Filippi, P., & Kostakis, V. (2017). Blockchain and value systems in the sharing economy: The illustrative case of Backfeed. *Technological Forecasting and Social Change*, 125, 105–15.

Pennington, R., Wilcox, H. D., & Grover, V. (2003). The role of system trust in business-to-consumer transactions. *Journal of Management Information Systems*, 20(3), 197–226.

Pereira, J., Tavalaei, M. M., & Ozalp, H. (2019). Blockchain-based platforms: Decentralized infrastructures and its boundary conditions. *Technological Forecasting and Social Change*, 146, 94–102.

Pinkham, B. C., & Peng, M. W. (2017). Overcoming institutional voids via arbitration. *Journal of International Business Studies*, 48(3), 344–59.

Poole, J. (2016). *Textbook on Contract Law*. New York: Oxford University Press.

Poppo, L., & Zenger, T. (2002). Do formal contracts and relational governance function as substitutes or complements? *Strategic Management Journal*, 23 (8), 707–25.

Puranam, P. (2018). *The Microstructure of Organizations*. Oxford: Oxford University Press.

Puranam, P., Alexy, O., & Reitzig, M. (2014). What's 'new' about new forms of organizing? *Academy of Management Review*, 39(2), 162–80.

PwC. (2020). PwC's global blockchain survey. Accessed 2 June 2021. www .pwc.com/gx/en/industries/technology/blockchain/blockchain-in-business .html.

Reuer, J. J., & Ariño, A. (2007). Strategic alliance contracts: Dimensions and determinants of contractual complexity. *Strategic Management Journal*, 28 (3), 313–30.

Roels, G., & Tang, C. S. (2017). Win-win capacity allocation contracts in coproduction and codistribution alliances. *Management Science*, 63(3), 861–81.

Rooney, K. (2021). Overall bitcoin-related crime fell last year, but one type of crypto hack is booming. *CNBC*. Accessed 30 July 2022. www.cnbc.com/2021/01/24/overall-bitcoin-related-crime-fell-last-year-but-one-type-of-crypto-hack-is-booming.html#:~:text=Last%20year%2 C%20illicit%20activity%20made,from%20blockchain%20data%20firm%20Chainalysis.&text=The%20category%20made%20up%20just,by%20311%25%20year%20over%20year.

Ryall, M. D., & Sampson, R. C. (2009). Formal contracts in the presence of relational enforcement mechanisms: Evidence from technology development projects. *Management Science*, 55(6), 906–25.

Saberi, S., Kouhizadeh, M., Sarkis, J., & Shen, L. (2019). Blockchain technology and its relationships to sustainable supply chain management. *International Journal of Production Research*, 57(7), 2117–35.

Salah, K., Rehman, M. H. U., Nizamuddin, N., & Al-Fuqaha, A. (2019). Blockchain for AI: Review and open research challenges. *IEEE Access*, 7, 10127–49.

Sampson, R. C. (2007). R&D alliances and firm performance: The impact of technological diversity and alliance organization on innovation. *Academy of Management Journal*, 50(2), 364–86.

Santos, F. M., & Eisenhardt, K. M. (2005). Organizational boundaries and theories of organization. *Organization Science*, 16(5), 491–508.

Schallbruch, M., & Skierka, I. (2018). Requirements for a German 'blockchain strategy'. *Digital Society Institute Berlin*. Accessed 22 April 2022. https://faculty-research.esmt.berlin/sites/faculty/files/2019-03/dsi-ipr_2018-3_en-de.pdf.

Schepker, D. J., Oh, W. Y., Martynov, A., & Poppo, L. (2014). The many futures of contracts: Moving beyond structure and safeguarding to coordination and adaptation. *Journal of Management*, 40(1), 193–225.

Schilke, O., & Cook, K. S. (2013). A cross-level process theory of trust development in interorganizational relationships. *Strategic Organization*, 11(3), 281–303.

Schilke, O., & Cook, K. S. (2015). Sources of alliance partner trustworthiness: Integrating calculative and relational perspectives. *Strategic Management Journal*, 36(2), 276–97.

Schilke, O., & Goerzen, A. (2010). Alliance management capability: An investigation of the construct and its measurement. *Journal of Management*, 36(5), 1192–219.

Schilke, O., & Lumineau, F. (2018). The double-edged effect of contracts on alliance performance. *Journal of Management*, 44(7), 2827–58.

Schilke, O., Reimann, M., & Cook, K. S. (2021). Trust in social relations. *Annual Review of Sociology*, 47, 239–59. https://doi.org/10.1146/annurev-soc-082120-082850.

Schilke, O., Wiedenfels, G., Brettel, M., & Zucker, L. G. (2017). Interorganizational trust production contingent on product and performance uncertainty. *Socio-Economic Review*, 15(2), 307–30.

Schmeiss, J., Hoelzle, K., & Tech, R. P. G. (2019). Designing governance mechanisms in platform ecosystems: Addressing the paradox of openness through blockchain technology. *California Management Review*, 62, 121–43.

Schmidt, C. G., & Wagner, S. M. (2019). Blockchain and supply chain relations: A transaction cost theory perspective. *Journal of Purchasing and Supply Management*, 25(4), 100552.

Schwab, K. (2017). *The Fourth Industrial Revolution*. New York: Penguin Random House.

Selznick, P. (1957). *Leadership in Administration: A Sociological Interpretation*. Berkeley, CA: University of California Press.

Segal, E. (2021). What will the next decade bring? Here are 20 predictions from trend forecasters. *The Guardian*. Accessed 21 June 2021. www.theguardian .com/commentisfree/2021/feb/15/2020s-trend-predictions-forecasters-working-from-home-ai-climate.

Shackelford, S. J., & Myers, S. (2017). Block-by-block: Leveraging the power of blockchain technology to build trust and promote cyber peace. *Yale Journal of Law and Technology*, 19(1), 334–88.

Sharma, P., Paul, S., & Sharma, S. (2020). What's in a name? A lot if it has 'blockchain'. *Economics Letters*, 186, 108818.

Simon, H. A. (1957). *Models of Man: Social and Rational*. New York: Wiley.

Smith, A. (1776). *The Wealth of Nations*. New York: Alfred A. Knopf.

Spence, M. (1973). Job market signaling. *Quarterly Journal of Economics*, 87 (3), 355–74.

Standard Chartered. (2019). We've completed our first cross-border Letter of Credit blockchain transaction in the oil industry with PTT Group. Accessed 2 June 2021. www.sc.com/en/media/press-release/weve-completed-our-first-cross-border-letter-of-credit-blockchain-transaction-in-the-oil-industry-with-ptt-group/.

Statista. (2021). Cryptocurrency projects: Funds raised worldwide by industry 2019. Accessed 12 May 2021. www.statista.com/statistics/802925/world wide-amount-crytocurrency-ico-projects-by-industry/.

Sternberg, H. S., Hofmann, E., & Roeck, D. (2021). The struggle is real: Insights from a supply chain blockchain case. *Journal of Business Logistics*, 42(1), 71–87.

Sulkowski, A. (2018). Blockchain, business supply chains, sustainability, and law: The future of governance, legal frameworks, and lawyers. *Delaware Journal of Corporate Law*, 43(2), 303–45.

Sundarakani, B., Ajaykumar, A., & Gunasekaran, A. (2021). Big data driven supply chain design and applications for blockchain: An action research using case study approach. *Omega*, 102, 102452.

Swanson, T. (2020). Blockchain: Enigma, paradox, opportunity. *Deloitte.* Accessed 21 June 2021. www2.deloitte.com/content/dam/Deloitte/uk/Documents/Innovation/deloitte-uk-blockchain-key-challenges.pdf.

Szabo, N. (1997). Smart contracts: Formalizing and securing relationships on public networks. *First Monday*, 2(9). https://doi.org/10.5210/fm.v2i9.548.

Tanwar, S., Parekh, K., & Evans, R. (2020). Blockchain-based electronic healthcare record system for healthcare 4.0 applications. *Journal of Information Security and Applications*, 50, 102407.

The Economist. (2015). The promise of the blockchain: The trust machine. Accessed 30 July 2022. www.economist.com/leaders/2015/10/31/the-trust-machine

Torres de Oliveira, R., Indulska, M., & Zalan, T. (2020). Guest editorial: Blockchain and the multinational enterprise: Progress, challenges and future research avenues. *Review of International Business and Strategy*, 30(2), 145–61.

Trabucchi, D., Moretto, A., Buganza, T., & MacCormack, A. (2020). Disrupting the disruptors or enhancing them? How blockchain reshapes two-sided platforms. *Journal of Product Innovation Management*, 37(6), 552–74.

Treiblmaier, H. (2018). The impact of the blockchain on the supply chain: A theory-based research framework and a call for action. *Supply Chain Management: An International Journal*, 23(6), 545–59.

Tsolakis, N., Niedenzu, D., Simonetto, M., Dora, M., & Kumar, M. (2021). Supply network design to address United Nations Sustainable Development Goals: A case study of blockchain implementation in Thai fish industry. *Journal of Business Research*, 131, 495–519.

U.S. Department of Justice. (2021). Department of Justice seizes $2.3 million in cryptocurrency paid to the ransomware extortionists darkside. Accessed 18 June 2021. www.justice.gov/opa/pr/department-justice-seizes-23-million-cryptocurrency-paid-ransomware-extortionists-darkside.

van der Scheer, W. (2018). How blockchain leads to new organizational structures. *Xebia.* Accessed 18 June 2021. https://articles.xebia.com/how-blockchain-leads-to-new-organizational-structures.

van Hoek, R. (2019). Exploring blockchain implementation in the supply chain. *International Journal of Operations & Production Management*, 39(6), 829–59.

van Pelt, R. V., Jansen, S., Baars, D., & Overbeek, S. (2021). Defining blockchain governance: A framework for analysis and comparison. *Information Systems Management*, 38(1), 21–41.

Vergne, J. P. (2020). Decentralized vs. distributed organization: Blockchain, machine learning and the future of the digital platform. *Organization Theory*, 1(4), 1–26. https://doi.org/10.1177/2631787720977052.

Vigliotti, M. G., & Jones, H. (2020). *The Executive Guide to Blockchain*. Cham: Palgrave Macmillan.

Volberda, H. W. (1996). Toward the flexible form: How to remain vital in hypercompetitive environments. *Organization Science*, 7(4), 359–74.

Wang, S., & Vergne, J. P. (2017). Buzz factor or innovation potential: What explains cryptocurrencies' returns? *PLoS One*, 12(1), e0169556. https://doi.org/10.1371/journal.pone.0169556.

Wang, W., Hoang, D. T., Hu, P. et al. (2019). A survey on consensus mechanisms and mining strategy management in blockchain networks. *IEEE Access*, 7, 22328–70.

Werbach, K. (2018). *The Blockchain and the New Architecture of Trust*. Cambridge, MA: MIT Press.

Williamson, O. E. (1975). *Market and Hierarchies: Antitrust Implications*. New York: Free Press.

Williamson, O. E. (1985). *The Economic Institutions of Capitalism*. New York: Free Press.

Williamson, O. E. (1996). *The Mechanisms of Governance*. New York: Oxford University Press.

Wood, D. J., & Gray, B. (1991). Toward a comprehensive theory of collaboration. *The Journal of Applied Behavioral Science*, 27(2), 139–62.

Xia, Q. I., Sifah, E. B., Asamoah, K. O. et al. (2017). MeDShare: Trust-less medical data sharing among cloud service providers via blockchain. *IEEE Access*, 5, 14757–67.

Xu, J., Wang, S., Bhargava, B. K., & Yang, F. (2019). A blockchain-enabled trustless crowd-intelligence ecosystem on mobile edge computing. *IEEE Transactions on Industrial Informatics*, 15(6), 3538–47.

Yang, C. S. (2019). Maritime shipping digitalization: Blockchain-based technology applications, future improvements, and intention to use. *Transportation Research Part E: Logistics and Transportation Review*, 131, 108–17.

Yin, H. H. S., Langenheldt, K., Harlev, M., Mukkamala, R. R., & Vatrapu, R. (2019). Regulating cryptocurrencies: A supervised machine learning approach to de-anonymizing the bitcoin blockchain. *Journal of Management Information Systems*, 36(1), 37–73.

Yoon, J., Talluri, S., Yildiz, H., & Sheu, C. (2020). The value of blockchain technology implementation in international trades under demand volatility risk. *International Journal of Production Research*, 58(7), 2163–83.

Yu, Y., Huang, G., & Guo, X. (2021). Financing strategy analysis for a multi-sided platform with blockchain technology. *International Journal of Production Research*, 59(15), 4513–32.

Yuthas, K., Sarason, Y., & Aziz, A. (2021). Strategic value creation through enterprise blockchain. *Journal of the British Blockchain Association*, 4(1). https://doi.org/10.31585/jbba-4-1-(7)2021.

Zalan, T. (2018). Born global on blockchain. *Review of International Business and Strategy*, 28(1), 19–34.

Zand, D. E. (1972). Trust and managerial problem solving. *Administrative Science Quarterly*, 17(2), 229–39.

Zavolokina, L., Ziolkowski, R., Bauer, I., & Schwabe, G. (2020). Management, governance and value creation in a blockchain consortium. *MIS Quarterly Executive*, 19(1), 1–17.

Zhao, X., Ai, P., Lai, F., Luo, X., & Benitez, J. (2022). Task management in decentralized autonomous organization. *Journal of Operations Management*, forthcoming. https://doi.org/10.1002/joom.1179.

Zhou, K. Z., & Poppo, L. (2010). Exchange hazards, relational reliability, and contracts in China: The contingent role of legal enforceability. *Journal of International Business Studies*, 41(5), 861–81.

Zhou, K. Z., & Xu, D. (2012). How foreign firms curtail local supplier opportunism in China: Detailed contracts, centralized control, and relational governance. *Journal of International Business Studies*, 43(7), 677–92.

Ziolkowski, R., Miscione, G., & Schwabe, G. (2020). Decision problems in blockchain governance: Old wine in new bottles or walking in someone else's shoes? *Journal of Management Information Systems*, 37(2), 316–48.

Zucker, L. G. (1986). Production of trust: Institutional sources of economic structure, 1840 to 1920, in Cummings, L. L., & Staw, M. (eds.), *Research in Organizational Behavior*, vol. 8. Greenwich, CT: JAI Press, 53–112.

# Acknowledgements

We thank the editor J.-C. Spender for his guidance and helpful suggestions. We also thank Andrea Contigiani, Yongcheng Fu, Marvin Hanisch, Ying-Ying Hsieh, Clotilde Landais, Arvind Malhotra, Alex Murray, Jean-Philippe Vergne, and Sophia Zhang for their insights and comments on earlier versions of the manuscript. All errors remain the authors' own.

Cambridge Elements $\equiv$

# Business Strategy

## Elements in the Series

*Corporate Social Responsibility*
Christopher Wickert and David Risi

*Agent-Based Strategizing*
Duncan A. Robertson

*Austrian Perspectives on Management: Entrepreneurship, Strategy, and Organization*
Nicolai J. Foss, Peter G. Klein and Matthew McCaffrey

*Microfoundations: Nature, Debate, and Promise*
Nicolai J. Foss and Stefan Linder

*High Velocity Business Operations*
Yemmanur Jayachandra

*Strategy Consulting*
Jeroen Kraaijenbrink

*Tools for Strategy: A Starter Kit for Academics and Practitioners*
Henri Hakala and Tero Vuorinen

*What Every CEO Should Know About AI*
Viktor Dörfler

*Dynamic Capabilities: History and an Extension*
Bart Nooteboom

*Knowledge Strategies*
Constantin Bratianu

*Blockchains: Strategic Implications for Contracting, Trust, and Organizational Design*
Wenqian Wang, Fabrice Lumineau and Oliver Schilke

A full series listing is available at: www.cambridge.org/EBUS

Printed in the United States
by Baker & Taylor Publisher Services